The Art of
Not Getting Lost
on the Way
Home

Journeying well with God, despite life's questions

DR VANGJEL SHORE

RIVER
PUBLISHING

River Publishing & Media Ltd
Barham Court
Teston
Maidstone
Kent
ME18 5BZ
United Kingdom

info@river-publishing.co.uk

ISBN 978-1-908393-31-9
Printed in the United Kingdom
Cover design by www.SpiffingCovers.com

Contents

Dedication

To Ben and Lani; Amy and Seng,
for consistently challenging me as your
father to keep growing up!

Acknowledgements

To all who accepted the invitation to commence the journey in *The Art of Not Disappearing*, thank you for your many encouragements and for sharing what God is doing in your lives through the book.

As I continue to take brave new steps to let go of the familiar and the certain, to my astonishment, I have found that this strange new world I have entered has actually introduced me to new friends, nourishing conversations and noteworthy inspiration so that I could finish this second book. Therefore, "a Huge Thank you" to...

Gloria, for making real to me, God's reckless generosity; David, for being "a presence-carrier"; Daniel, for sittings and storytelling at St Arbucks; Chris and Sarah, at home in your hearts; Graeme, for the gift of friendship; Rob, for consistent integrity; Sharon and Patrick, for practical kindnesses; Sue, for being naturally supernatural; Tim and Jonathan, for belief and patience; Jude, "right is rite"; Margaret and Kang Hoe, for faith, hope and love; and Heazle: "VTR alive in you, empowers me to laugh, lament and love fully with you..."

Introduction

But if heaven never was promised to me,
neither God's promise to live eternally...
neither a land where we'll never grow old...
It's been worth...having the Lord in my life.
(Andrae Crouch, 1972)[1]

I vividly recall the first time that I heard the lyrics of the song quoted above. Its smooth and soulful delivery held my attention, and I memorised it. It seemed easy enough to sing, but it was more than a song. It was a summons to examine my motives for following Jesus. Because once the lyrics got under my skin and into the crevices of my soul, I began to see something about the radical nature of Christianity.

You cannot consign Jesus to some era of ancient history. It is said that you cannot keep a good man down, and Jesus was more than a man. Because of him, life, death, heaven, hell, love, hate, faith, hope and religion undergo a massive overhaul. This kind of renovation catapults us into a space where in light of the lyrics we ask:

Could I really stay the distance with Jesus if there were no promise of heaven?

Could I remain true to Jesus to the very end, even if it meant that the prize was not living eternally?

Deep down, I knew that it was not just my mind playing tricks with me. Somehow the bigger reality of God was breaking through to the much smaller world of me. I certainly had signed up to follow Jesus, yet now I needed to answer the song's challenge.

Don Williams says that, 'The journey is the destination.' Of course, that destination is heaven. 'So, I'm on my way to heaven, we shall not be moved,' and the beat goes on. However,

What if Christianity offered no other incentive but Jesus, from start to finish?

What if every step of faith in following Jesus meant allowing God to make his home or be at home in me right now?

The title of this book, *The Art of Not Getting Lost on the Way Home*, can only make sense to us if we know what constitutes our true home. It must transcend the physical and geographical sphere of our lives, and even the arena of family and relatives. In the Christian tradition, heaven cannot be dismissed. Yet there is so much more going on in this faith journey with God who is our ultimate home.

In other words, if all I want is to get out of this messy world so that I can spend eternity in heaven, then I am short-sighted and narrow-minded. I am also denying myself the immense privilege of allowing God to bring heaven through me into this present world. If I can learn to be at home now with the very One who is our home, it will allow others to taste and see, and find their way to their true home with God.

God wants to make his home in me now so that I will discover what it means to be finally living for the first time. He is committed to teaching us how to live now, and not just when all that is evil – all that pertains to sin, Satan and everything that turns us away from God – is out of the picture. It is right now that God wants us to infuse this present world with heaven's reality. His heart aches for every human being to experience heaven breaking into this present age. Heaven's light and love all emanate from God, Father, Son and Holy Spirit, whose desire it is to be at home with us and us with him, on earth as it is in heaven.

We need a certain reverent and humble agnosticism about the precise nature of hell, as about the precise nature of heaven. Both are beyond our understanding. But clear and definite we must be that hell is an awful, eternal reality. It is not dogmatism that is unbecoming in speaking about the fact of hell; it is glibness and frivolity. How can we think about hell without tears?

It is fascinating that the last document in the New Testament actually depicts heaven as coming down to us. Could it be that followers of Jesus have spent too much time trying to get people to heaven rather than bringing heaven to them right now?

Heaven invading earth is literally being sustained by Jesus, 'the bread of life' and the 'the living water' right now. Our hunger and thirst can be fully met in Jesus, because not only is he the One that nourishes us in our long journey of faith, but he also is the hunger and the thirst in us to be satisfied with nothing else and no one else but him!

Tom Wright is definitely onto something when he speaks of these days as the 'first days, and not so much the last days'. In effect, God has already invaded this world and initiated a new beginning with a new humanity. A fresh start for everybody can become a reality precisely because of Jesus. God wants us to know that we can passionately live out these last days as if they were 'the first days' of what heaven and earth combined would be like, with God at home in human lives surrendered to him.

Unquestionably, the human heart has a longing to be at home;

to be somewhere or with someone. It is being found, being heard, being held, being known, being seen, being aware of being at home. It is not about being controlled. Being at home with God affirms the privilege of becoming an authentic human being and reflecting the very nature of who he is in this world which we are passing through.

After writing my first book *The Art of Not Disappearing*,[2] my wife Heazle asked me what it felt like to have accomplished such a huge challenge. My response surprised not only her, but also myself. I said that 'It feels like I have written myself out of a box.' Little did I realise what I was saying with those words.

Just think, we may all eventually leave this old world in a box, yet God is actually trying to get us out of the box right now! A box represents anything which confines us to a shallow and small-minded life without God. It is anything aligning us to a way of thinking that leaves us smaller as persons and lost to everything else but God.

In November 2010, five minutes before submitting my resignation from my job, I sat quietly at my desk. For a brief moment I closed my eyes and consciously recalled the conversations and stories which had transpired in my office. Their loud echoes were interspersed with unceasing waves of images. Faces of people emerged, stained with bitter tears. They were people fighting desperately to articulate their unattended sorrow and pain.

Conversely, there were faces glistening with hope. I remember the lady with the racoon eyes. Her mascara clearly had a mind of its own, moving from its original location to paint its own design on her face. Tears have a way of taking you to places where you may not want to be or even where you know you need to be.

Then it was that I opened my eyes and was alerted to a small daily devotional book on the corner of the shelf. Half-hidden by the larger volumes, it seemed to invite me to pick it up and read.

Immediately, I got out of my chair and opened it to that day's date. The headline verse was clear and uncomplicated: *'Get up. Let's go. It's time to leave here'* (John 14:31). I felt God laugh with me.

Nonetheless, uncertainty, like thunder booming in the sky, made its presence known to me. The world of the familiar, of friends and foes, of relationships, routines, rituals and home comforts, was intersecting with a brand new world which would represent the unfamiliar and unexplored. And yet the moment I stuttered, 'yes' to God, he responded immediately. His revelation brought formation to my restless spirit, directing it to remember Abraham, Jesus and another much loved story...

By an act of faith, Abraham said yes to God's call to travel to an unknown place that would become his home. When he left he had no idea where he was going.

Jesus said, 'Anyone who intends to come with me has to let me lead. You're not in the driver's seat, I am...' (Mark 8:34)

And larger than life, there was Bilbo Baggins telling Gandalf, 'I love my six square meals a day and my Hobbit hole' (translate 'box' for me). Gandalf the Wise One summons Bilbo to prepare for a long and arduous venture, and awkwardly, Bilbo capitulates.

Like Abraham and Bilbo Baggins, I was clueless as to this faith venture. And the first step taken would mean learning earlier rather than later, that Jesus must be in the driver's seat and not me. Therefore: 'Get up. Let's go. It's time to leave here,' gave traction for my new venture with Jesus.

So it was that in January 2011, my wife Heazle and I both left our secure jobs and the shorelines of Australia, and accepted an invitation to come away and live in Asia. Neither of us had specific positions to go to, only the generous invitation to come and be in the company of two people who love and believe in us. We had not daily shared our lives with our daughter and son-in-law for a number of years, and they would now allow us to see what life would be like out of the box.

Following Jesus sounds quite simple: 'Follow me!' However, integral to that challenge is learning to let go of everything. The scary truth is that when we begin this venture with Jesus, our understanding of faith gets vacuumed and cleaned so that we end up with something that appears very fragile. This overhaul is destabilising and disorienting. We have to grasp that faith is not for overcoming obstacles, but for experiencing them all the way to the end of the journey.

In the midst of the instability and disorientation, we must learn to see God at work. When we begin to be honest with God and ourselves, not only do we see better, but we listen better. We realise how numbed we have become to the groaning of our spirit, oblivious to its deepest sigh: 'Is this all there is?'

This book is an outcome not only of the first step to leave, but also of the many steps which have followed in finding my true home. *The Art of Not Getting Lost on the Way Home* builds on my first book in continuing to challenge us to accept the 'gift of our true selves, our child-of-God selves'. They both celebrate the truth of our incarnational reality in Jesus: namely, becoming an authentic human being who is fully alive and fully present to God, self and others.

The first chapter confronts us with a question which I have heard expressed in a thousand and one different settings. I have hurled it in God's face with clenched fists. I have heard it vented in hard cold logic. I have felt all the venom one person could muster in their entire life when used. It is a question which is no respecter of persons, religious or irreligious, position or place. It just is. It sounds like: 'O God, where the hell are you?'

Our quest to find an answer locates us in the Hebrew scriptures, especially the prophet Isaiah. By doing some excavation we will glean insights which can lead us out of our sense of lostness, and change what has impacted our outlook on life and our relationship with God. Its purpose is to inspire us to hold onto God, with or without an answer to our hard questions.

The second chapter explores the question, 'O God, why can't I know everything right now?' Our desire to know is definitely God-given, but there is a darker side to knowing which does not always lead to positive transformation into being an authentic person. This chapter pushes us to explore our relationship with God.

I call God the enigmatic educator. He is puzzling, perplexing and always urging us to learn to navigate his pathways. By sifting through the discomforting scenario of the first humans in the garden, we are not only able to unmask the tempter, and stay true to God and ourselves, but slowly begin to grasp the difference between the paradox and the parody of knowing. After all, there can only be one know-it-all in the Universe, and last I checked, the throne of heaven is not vacant...

The third chapter is simply titled, 'O God, what are you trying to tell me?' Here we trace the journey of a Jewish theologian who encounters the rabbi from Nazareth. He has to face the challenge of getting out of his box. He finds himself drawn into the far bigger mystery of God than he can work out by study. His journey takes him further and deeper than he has ever been before. Step by step, however, we see vulnerability, transparency and responsibility as God's grace-gifts to this seeker. This man discovers how to come home to God by being at home with himself and Jesus.

The fourth chapter poses the question, 'O God, is this really you?' It challenges us to be prepared to be both startled and surprised when it comes to the diversity of ways in which God chooses to reveal himself to us. It is fascinating that the Hebrew word for 'presence' is often conveyed in the plural. In English, the Hebrew word conveys the idea of 'face,' but because it is plural it denotes 'faces.' People and life circumstances are often God's way of coming to us up close and personal with his many faces.

God is not to be stereotyped, and he refuses to conform to the image we want him to be for us and our agenda. How often have we been caught out by the fact that God has been there all along and we did not even notice? This is why our question, 'O God, is this really you?' matters. If we are to allow ourselves to be found by him, it means allowing God to deal with our opinionated hearts and hard heads, so that we do not get lost in our religious thing.

'O God, will I really make it?' sums up the final chapter. It invites us to examine where we are headed and what our understanding of home really is. There is a conspicuous absence of Jesus' usage of heaven as home. Surprisingly, Jesus often referred to the end of his journey as returning to his Father.

For Jesus, home is best represented as being with his Father. Heaven is not dismissed, but our understanding of being at home with God, only adds to the wonder of all that God has for his children, right now and not just later on. This is especially so in relation to living life and keeping in step with our very own personal tutor, the Holy Spirit.

The Art of Not Getting Lost on the Way Home is more than a book title. The basic thesis of this book is that 'home' principally represents being at home with God right now. By using questions to frame the chapters of this book, I intend to ignite fresh faith, inspire flagging hope, and infuse longing love in us.

My desire is that not only will we stay the distance with Jesus, but also, that heaven's reality and our earthly existence become one, intentionally, experientially and of course ultimately in the new heavens and the new earth.

Endnotes
1. Andrae Crouch, 'If heaven were never promised to me', Just Andrae, 1972
2. The Art of Not Disappearing (River Publishing, 2011)

Chapter One
'O God, Where The Hell Are You?'

The night was gone.
The morning star was shining in the sky.
I too had become a completely different person.

The student of the Talmud, the child that I was,
had been consumed in the flames.
There remained only a shape that looked like me.

A dark flame had entered into my soul and devoured it.
I did not deny God's existence,
but I doubted his absolute justice
(Elie Wiesel)[1]

My observation about people from all walks of life and all manner of religious categories is that 'O God, where the hell are you?' is not always a one-off outburst. Life never turns out as we had imagined; it makes up its own mind. Our best-laid plans and well-rehearsed scripts do not always bring the outcomes we long for. Each of us has momentary flare-ups, either with gritted teeth or bated breath, clenched fists or clamorous outbursts, where we simply let God have it. We just want to tell him off.

It appears that God has left us stranded and lost. Even if we tell ourselves and others that we had heard from God, somehow there is no light for our darkness and no sense of hope in our despair. We have taken the appropriate action, ticked all the right boxes and yet, look at where we find ourselves. Deep down, where our nervous system cringes because we feel so alone, we bellow out, 'O God, where the hell are you?' 'God, you have not come through for us.'

For some it has been invective, for others, expletive, perhaps even a painful silence. Either way, this question respects neither the religious nor the irreligious.

Centuries before we ever found a place on the stage of human existence, a Jewish psalm writer and poet theologian called David said:

If I go up to the heavens, you are there;
If I make my bed in hell, behold, you are there. (Psalm 139:8)

In one breath, David informs us that there is a legitimate place to mention God and hell together. The Psalms disclose to us that God wants us to be heard. He wants us to know that we do have a voice. And although he enters into our pain with us, he does not indulge our self-pity.

Sometimes it seems like God is hearing-impaired, or refusing to deal with the presenting issues in our lives. However, what we may construe as inactivity on God's part, quite often does not mean that he is not at work. Rather, it has so much more to do with the way that he is working out his much larger purposes, which do include us, even if we are unable to handle his strange ways in our lives.

We must learn from our earliest days that God never misses the frequency of a human heart crying out to him. He remains utterly and absolutely present to us and for us in all situations. Therefore with each step we take in grasping what the poet is saying, we may find ourselves led into a bigger world, one much larger than our own. This larger world, even with its present darkness, is illuminated by one word in David's poem. And what a world of difference is contained in the English translation of the Hebrew word hinnêh – 'behold'!

For David there is the obvious expectation that yes, of course, God is in the heavens. Yet that tiny word 'behold' expresses a dimension of utter astonishment. It is like an exclamation mark. I am startled and surprised, baffled and bewildered, to find that when I make my bed in hell, behold, you are there as well.

It transcends poetic license when David gives voice to his innermost thought of hell, asserting, 'God, you are there'. This man was keenly aware of the realm of darkness and Sheol as he faced death on the battlefield as a mighty warrior-king. David's poignant words, *'Even though I walk through the valley of the shadow of death, I will not fear'* (Psalm 23:4) were not mere abstractions. His declaration, 'If I make my bed in hell, behold, you are there' is expressed with lucid thought and clarity of heart.

You, O God, can meet us in the brightest heavenly domain or the darkest hellish realm.

You, O God, can meet us in our deepest pain or shame.

You, O God, are not absent nor do you abscond.

You, O God, are utterly there for us and with us.

If we can discover God in our hells, beneath us, around us, holding us up and holding us together when we are sinking into a bottomless pit of our undoing, then we can find him anywhere.[2] Everything is true, if this is true. If this knowledge that God is present in our hellish existence is more than mere poetic licence, then we can embrace incomprehensible hope.

The reality of this hope finds greater meaning for us in the stories of two extraordinary people...

Getting out of the way

Without a shadow of a doubt these two people were daily confronted with the 'O God, where the hell are you?' questioning. Both endured the blackest of nights and the longest of days and yet each had quite differing responses to God. And rather than getting lost to the chaotic darkness and seemingly interminable presence of evil, these two brave hearts stayed the course with God.

The first person we met in the opening quotation which introduced this chapter. His name is Elie Wiesel. His words defy imagination.

The night was gone.
The morning star was shining in the sky.
I too had become a completely different person.

The student of the Talmud, the child that I was, had been consumed in the flames.
There remained only a shape that looked like me.

A dark flame had entered into my soul and devoured it.
I did not deny God's existence, but I doubted his absolute justice.

Such words could only have been formed in the crucible of deep anguish and utter despair at the sheer evil that he and his fellow inmates witnessed daily. Romanian-born Elie Wiesel eloquently and honestly expresses the struggle of his faith journey with God. As a boy he was sent to Auschwitz and then Buchenwald, where both his parents and sister died.

He wrestled all his life with God to make sense of his experiences in the context of his Jewish faith, and continues to embrace it to this day, knowing that in true Jewish fashion, having it out with God is a given. Wiesel has attempted to tackle the 'O God, where the hell are you?' question in both human suffering and in God's apparent silence.

Wiesel has not let God off the hook. He understands this is one of the enduring mysteries with which men and women of faith have struggled over the centuries. Listen again to another painful memory from this Holocaust survivor and Nobel Laureate:

Then came the march past the victims.
The two men were no longer alive.
Their tongues were hanging out, swollen and bluish.

But the third rope was still moving: the child, too light, was still breathing...
And so he remained for more than half an hour,
lingering between life and death, writhing before our eyes.

And we were forced to look at him at close range.
He was still alive when I passed him.
His tongue was still red, his eyes not yet extinguished.

Behind me, I heard the same man asking:
'For God's sake, where is God?'
And from within me, I heard a voice answer:
'Where he is? This is where – hanging here from this gallows.'[3]

Wiesel's words graphically attempt to not only interpret his world amidst the unimaginable atrocities of the torture camps, but to capture his agony with God and humanity.

Questions are not, nor cannot be seen as superfluous in the faith journey. They are indispensable and must not be snuffed out. Even when the pain is unrelenting and the torment so terrifying, God cannot be let off the hook. Elie Wiesel had been introduced to this God in his early years by his parents, and through his pen we can glean much.

Whatever faith meant to Wiesel, it certainly transcended having all the right answers to the Catechism and doctrinal statement of his own tradition. It underscored the truth that faith is more than that which helps us to overcome obstacles. Faith is ours to experience all the way through to the very end of our human stories with God. Faith is keeping on believing in God and with God.

On the one hand, if we remain silent and allow injustice and evil to triumph, then we are not truly being human. We cannot make God accountable to us no matter how hard we try; nonetheless, Christians must with every inarticulate groan and unrelenting act of compassion make God credible in this world.

In all that Jesus embodied in his coming to this lonely planet, the most outrageous thought of all is that God grants us permission to make him credible in this world through human lives abandoned to Him.

Catholic novelist and journalist Francois Mauriac interviewed Elie Wiesel well after the war. Mauriac later wrote in the foreword to Night:

And I, who believe that God is love, what answer could I give my young questioner. What did I say to him? Did I speak of that other Israeli, his brother, who may have resembled him—the Crucified, whose cross has conquered the world? Did I affirm that the stumbling block to his faith was the cornerstone of mine and that the conformity between the cross and human suffering was in my eyes the key to that impenetrable mystery?[4]

Elie Wiesel chose not to get lost from God but chose to get lost in God, his true home.

Similarly, there is yet another who, enduring the nightmares of modern dictatorship and violence, made God credible by her resistance. This was Esther (Etty) Hillesum, a young Jewish woman in her twenties when the Germans occupied Holland. Although she did not have an explicit religious commitment, her published diaries and letters (1941-1943) shed light on how during this terrible period in the history of her country and her people, Etty became more and more conscious of God's hand on her life.

This was all the more remarkable at a time when many might have been more likely to feel deeply cynical about God, where faith could be abrogated and left to lay in the ruins of the war-torn villages dominating the landscape. Imprisoned in the transit camp at Westerbork before being shipped off to Auschwitz where she was to die in the gas chambers in November 1943 at the age of 29, Etty wrote,

There must be someone to live through it all and bear witness to the fact that God lived, even in these times. And why should I not be that witness?[5]

In a letter to a friend from Westerbork, Etty described her life as, 'having become an uninterrupted dialogue with you, O God.'[6] Her diaries also highlight her growing awareness of her sense of vocation in the camp:

As being not...simply to proclaim you, God, to commend you to the heart of others. One must also clear the path toward you in them.[7]

Etty's spiritual journey moved her more and more into the certainty that God gave her a place in his world of uncertainty. She must occupy that place where others could connect with God through her. Relentlessly, Etty took responsibility for God's believability. Rather than push him away, Etty allowed herself to be at home with God. She knew that this would mean pain as well as comfort; utter weakness as well as strength; hope and hopelessness clashing like cymbals, orchestrated by hands not always her own.

Both Elie Wiesel and Etty Hillesum were writing in exceptional times. Faith for these two people was lost and found, shattered and unearthed, forged and tempered in the fiery furnaces of untold atrocities and unrequited dignity. Each in their own way was caught up in a God-reality which they could neither deny nor ignore. Neither was reticent nor reluctant to tackle God – answers or no answers – in their abhorrent hell. They stayed true, without allowing everything in their lives to sabotage faith, hope and love in the God who knew them and heard them.

Is this what being at home with God really looks like?

Is this how we learn the art of not getting lost on the way home?

They both sought to get out of the way and at the same time be in his way, so that God could continue with his purposes in their lives. Both Wiesel and Hillesum, as well as the many unnamed strugglers before and after them, bear witness to unprecedented brutality and unparalleled bewilderment while holding on to the God who is not absent. Their stories of the anguish and utter despair, the violence and despotism, the hope and hopelessness, bring to mind stories from the Hebrew Scriptures.

The road to tomorrow leads through yesterday[8]

The Hebrew Scriptures record how God dealt with the tribes of ancient Israel over a period of well over a thousand years. However, for any keen students of the Bible, the prophetic books stand clearly apart among all the genres. Two reasons come to mind:

The combination of proclamation, politics and poetry in the prophetic books leave theological, historical and literary commentators speechless. Theme upon theme and layer upon layer of prophetic literature resist anything too neatly ordered, and yet all derive from the same source, namely, God. Secondly, what is of keen interest to us is that prophetic literature emphasizes the self-disclosure of God.[9] This is of paramount importance as we probe his character in relation to the question: 'O God, where the hell are you?'

From end to end, chapter by chapter, the landscape of the Hebrew Scriptures is not only an encounter with the immensity of God, but also with the stark reality of loss. It is true to say that creativity and faith cannot emerge unless loss is examined and explored. When our losses are explored, then we can be gifted with unimaginable gains. These findings can help us to learn to be at home with God in the midst of all that cannot be worked out or answered.

Losses will always remain such when we do not crawl out from under the covers of defeat and despair, darkness and death. Yet all our tomorrows can be interpreted through the lens of our yesterdays as we hungrily ingest God's word and the wonder of his presence. The answers may not always be immediate or those we had hoped for, yet hope is being born.

And hope is born of memory. When memory submits to being baptized by the word and Spirit of God, then we may continue our faith journey, stumbling, yet resolutely aware that God remains God and is committed to us for the long haul of coming home.

If we are in too much of a hurry to extricate ourselves from the world of God's word, we may forfeit being captured by its identity-forming stories which have inherent power to transform our faith. Even though the 'O God, where the hell are you?' outburst is not a quotation from Scripture, the expression resonates with those who find themselves in the womb of exile.

Biblical scholars agree that the Babylonian exile began one of the most fertile periods of Israelite writing.[10] It forcefully reminds us that even when God appears to be absent, two elements defiantly beckon us to look with new eyes: That even God appears to be foolish enough to dream a new future for himself and his world, and its language stirs us forward out of our denial and despair in order to push us into the place of hope and expectation in God.

What is true of the prophets is equally true of the cathartic utterances of the Psalms. They are an honest and courageous practice of prayer. Psalms offer the bright prospect for turning brutalizing loss and a sense of abandonment into an act of faith that can deliver promise and a hope. They capture and craft an authentic voice that appeals to God's character to be heard and to be found. Prophets or psalm writers enable us to identify, recount, name, and legitimize our grief.

Psalms were sung. However, they are devoid of any specific musical notation. Could it be that God wants us to find our own authentic voice to sing them?

I have noticed that people remember songs more than they do sermons and speeches. As we gather publicly in church, we can sing about our grief, our doubts, our triumphs, and even our losses. This public identification legitimates our feelings. For this very reason, ruthless honesty about our past and present faith journey empowers us to say with the future in focus:

"God, you gave me permission to make you credible in my human narrative. How else will others come to trust you and know you as the only true God?"

We are here: Where are you?

From her earliest inception, God summoned Israel to a journey of spiritual significance. God was on the move with his people and Israel's faith found great resolve in the unwavering bedrock truth that

His works are perfect, and the way he works is fair and just. A God you can depend upon, no exceptions, a straight-arrow God. His messed up, mixed up children, his non children, throw mud at him but none of it sticks. (Deuteronomy 32:4)

...it was your ancestors that God fell in love with, he picked their children – that's you – out of all the other peoples. (Deuteronomy 10:15)

Is it any wonder that with such a formidable revelation of unfailing dependency and reliability, Israel felt entirely special being chosen by this God?

Yet as any theological or Bible college graduate soon discovers, degrees can only take you so far in understanding God and his ways. Rather shockingly everything changed for the nation of Israel. Her stubborn refusal to heed the purposes and promises of God caused her to remain entrenched in self-interest and brought on the terrible moment of truth in 587 BC.

In that year Jerusalem was burned and its temple destroyed, the king was exiled, the leading citizens were deported and public life ended. For ancient Israel, it was the end of privilege, certitude, domination, viable public institutions and a sustaining social fabric. It was the end of life with God, which Israel had taken for granted. In that gut wrenching time, ancient Israel faced the temptation of denial—the pretence that there had been no loss—and it faced the temptation of despair—the inability to see any way out.[11]

For Israel, 'God, we are here, now, where the hell are you?' came to the fore. She found herself in a place she wouldn't have chosen. All that had shaped Israel's worldview as the people of God was now been brought into question, and especially, God's character.

Perhaps we too are where we don't want to be. We'd like to push the rewind button and get back to a different time. But as much as we'd like to be there, we can't be, because we've been exiled from that place. The landmarks are different. Everything feels strange. We are not only far from home, but also seemingly lost to all that our God had promised.

Exile is perhaps not a word which would so easily come to our lips today. The word we are much more familiar with would be refugee.

Our global village confronts us on a daily basis with the hundreds of thousands of men, women and children flung out and cast off into places of deep disorder, the outcome of not only natural disasters like famine and flood but also, repressive regimes. These dislocated people are stripped of their country, their sense of belonging or identity, and their human dignity.[12]

Have you ever wondered about the dissonance of despair in the refugee camps of our world?

Does the 'O God, where the hell are you?' sentiment reach an unparalleled and frightening crescendo?

If there is to be any consensus of solidarity with humanity in our chaotic world, especially in light of the interminable groaning of twenty-first century refugees, then the prophetic voice of C S Lewis needs to pin our ears back:

"God... shouts in our pains: it is his megaphone to rouse a deaf world."

Incredible as it seems, somehow our world appears to be much more sensitised to the uncertain fate of whales and the panda bear, than to the cry of fellow human beings that we encounter on a daily basis. In addition, the sheer complexity of the refugee crisis broadcasts the foreboding nature of exile and confronts us with a revelation.

In our impotence we can acquiesce to a foetal position and do nothing, or we can adopt a forceful posture of passionate prayer and exploits of compassionate acts. Our world is toxic in the most comprehensive sense. And we must declare that God has not abandoned this world, rather,

"God descends, not to eliminate the pain, but to be fully present in the midst of it. The Eternal is brought out of contradiction."[13]

The Israelites for centuries had the enduring status of the people of God, but now their new classification was that of refugee. Israel would spend seventy years in Babylon with a deepening sense of being forgotten by God, which siphoned off her hope of justice and of wrongs being righted.

The Hebrew Scriptures voice how devastating was the loss, and how great was the consequent fear of being without God's presence or activity. Israel's need to call God to account is understandable. And yet she had to fully recover the truth that her groans, sighs and supplications, prayers and praise were heard by the God from whom no secret can be kept.

With Israel of old and all humanity, God is relentless about transforming our terminal deception. We do not realise just how accomplished we have become in being fugitives from ourselves, especially when it comes to us and God. When we merely play out a religious performance, we are unable to fully appreciate the true roles of faith, hope and love.

These three graces can lead us in our journey of on-going transformation to our ultimate consummation where loss and grief, denial and despair, death and darkness shall be no more.

For the interim however, we must learn the art of not getting ourselves lost because we somehow have assumed that God is lost.

Isaiah: mediator and messenger

Long, long before our time, the Hebrew prophet Isaiah found himself with the assignment of mediating between God and Israel. Admittedly that's what prophets should be doing anyway, nonetheless his assignment was unenviable. Although God was fully aware of Israel's predicament, she was lamenting that he had forgotten her, rejected her and exiled her to Babylon. Therefore, Isaiah had to represent the petition of both the claimant and God.

What we soon discover is that God has left himself wide open to the exiles' accusations and vilifications. Exiles are characteristically stripped of all else except speech. What exiles do is to speak their mother tongue...as a way to maintain identity in a situation that is identity denying.[14]

Israel was not mute and would not let God off the hook. Her displacement by Yahweh, Lord of the covenant, created a cluster of excruciating issues: Not only was there a fundamental loss of control, but also no demonstrable hope of either a return to the past or an arrival at some future desired place, namely, home.

The prophet's remedy for Israel's mood of 'O God, where the hell are you?' is to remind her of two unalterable facts, namely, who God is and who Israel is. Combined, they give perspective in terms of both illumination and intervention.

His opening words to exiled Israel are to prepare themselves for his coming to them as their King (Isaiah 40:2-3). As much as this would engender hope of rescue, hope could only ever become a reality if Israel were willing to listen:

I don't think the way you think...and the way you work isn't the way I work. (Isaiah 55:8-9)

If our faith is just about certainty and always getting the right answers to our prayers, we may have to face the reality we have not truly met God. If anything, our conception of God has been almost entirely built with materials fixated on making him conform to what we want 'god' to be for us and our happiness. Similarly, it also confirms just how lost we have become.

'To whom then will you liken me and make me equal and compare me, that we may be alike?' (Isaiah 46:5)

Thus God, The Holy One of Israel, Israel's Maker, says, 'Do you question who or what I'm making? Are you telling me what I cannot do? I made earth, and I created man and woman to live on it and I handcrafted the skies and direct all the constellations in their turnings...'(Isaiah 45:12)

Isaiah portrays God as awesome in sovereignty and bewildering in mystery. Yet rather than leaving Israel feeling even more alienated and estranged at the magnitude of God's greatness, Isaiah suggests another perspective: God is immensely personal. He knows that Israel's exile challenges her ability to trust him, and his power and his presence with them. So the prophet reminds Israel:

Look at him! God, the Master, comes in power, ready to go into action.

He is going to pay back his enemies and reward those who have loved him.

Like a shepherd, he will care for his flock

Gathering the lambs in his arms,

Hugging them as he carries them

Leading the nursing ewes to good pasture. (Isaiah 40:11)

His word pictures convey how sheer grace will come through God's reckless self-disclosure to Israel in Babylon. It will transcend even what has been true of her history with him up to this point.[15] Israel will discover that God is never inactive. He is always at work in the world, with his people. History is fundamentally his story! Exile is his story. He is not absent. He definitely wants us to allow him to be at home with us, whatever shape we are in.

Israel has lost her way and she is very much in need of a thorough overhaul of her vision of God. And according to God's agenda, exile would prove to be the womb for such faith to be born, exposing the fallacious thinking that we can actually contribute anything to God. God is God and God remains God, even if we had never been created. So Israel's question: 'We are here now; where are you?' will begin to be answered as she learns to see with new eyes and hear with new ears God's message through Isaiah:

But I'll take the hand of those who don't know the way;

who can't see where they're going.

I'll be a personal guide to them,

directing them through unknown country.

I'll be right there to show them what roads to take,

make sure that they won't fall into the ditch.

These are the things that I'll be doing for them –
Sticking with them, not leaving them for a minute. (Isaiah 42:16)

Israel in exile is forcibly confronted with her own impotence and ignorance. We too face our own powerlessness, when we cannot deliver ourselves from a predicament. And ignorance: our protestations are often merely projections of where we think we should be according to our interpretation of the Scriptures which God has given. Everything appears to be so unknown, so uncertain. Just like Israel we must also learn that,

God has no use for the prayers of the people who won't listen to him. (Proverbs 28:9)

So the question, 'O God! Where the hell are you?' need not diminish our hunger and thirst for God. Rather, it surfaces our need to see where we truly are. Then we can begin to realise it is ok to stay clinging to God in the steep learning curve of being at home with him wherever we find ourselves in this world.

Biblical memory instructs us about our identity

But Zion said, 'I don't get it. God has left me. My Master has forgotten I even exist.' (Isaiah 49:14)

Here, 'Zion' is another word for ancient Israel. Israel was languishing in captivity in Babylon, and God picks up on her words of exasperation:

Why would you ever complain, O Jacob, or whine, Israel, saying, 'God has lost track of me. He doesn't care what happens to me?' (Isaiah 40:27)

Israel was aggrieved, yet deeply entrenched in her memory was God's covenant promise to make her as numerous as the stars, and a light and blessing to all the nations.[16] However in the culture of the ancient Near East, when one army conquered the forces of another nation and overthrew the temple of their god, that god was considered to be dead in history.

Jeremiah, a contemporary of Isaiah, captured the depth of Israel's painful anguish. He witnessed the captive Jews as they were forced to listen daily to the taunts of the Babylonians. His witness to the nadir of suffering is captured in his work, Lamentations. Israel had been overrun and intimidated and worst of all...

Is it that God had the power, but maybe he had lost the will to deliver them?

Over the years I have often had Christians ask me whether it is acceptable to complain to God. My response is usually three fold:

Yes, it is acceptable because God is big enough to handle anything we throw at him.

Yes, the Hebrew Scriptures give us permission to complain to God.

Yes, but are you really ready for what he has to say to *you* about *you*?

This permission is legitimized by the psalm maker David.

How long, O Lord?

Will you forget me forever?

How long will you hide your face from me?

How long must I wrestle with my thoughts

and day after day have sorrow in my heart?

...Look on me and answer, Lord my God. (Psalm 13:1-3)

We have the psalmist's permission to ask: How long, O Lord, will you forget me? David is pleading with God for the return of intimacy in his relationship with him. Yet this intimacy is nurtured in the truth that God's absence is not tied up in some thirty-day contractual arrangement of our need to be consistently consistent.

Nothing could be further from the truth.

God's memory does not work in response to our attempts to prod it. Rather it works in accordance with his character and purposes. Isaiah the prophet provides the following words of exhortation concerning who God is, for Israel's words of exasperation...

33

Words of exhortation

Do you not know? Have you not heard?
The Everlasting God, the Lord, the Creator of the ends of the earth,
does not become weary or tired.
His understanding is inscrutable. (Isaiah 40:28-29)

Isaiah, acting as mediator between the two parties, advises Israel to heed the following three unalterable truths concerning God:

1. God is everlasting: his power goes beyond time.

2. God is Creator of the ends of the earth: his power exceeds space.

3. Israel's plight is not due to God's lack of wisdom: his understanding is impenetrable.

Did you notice that Isaiah qualifies his words of exhortation with two searching questions?

'Do you not know?'

'And have you not heard?' (Isaiah 40:28)

The first question draws our attention to the matter of 'knowledge'

For Israel in Babylon, her knowledge base was heavily influenced by the encircling clouds of loss and grief, doubt and uncertainty, despair and isolation. All that represented her former status with God had been surrendered. These factors further compounded Israel's inability to both see and hear what was and what would always be true concerning herself and God.

Israel's dilemma was not only due to her unwillingness to apply what she knew about God in her situation, but also, her own need to deal with why she was in exile in the first place. In Israel's history, God had previously spoken to her leaders and kings...

But if you or your sons betray me, ignoring my guidance and judgments, taking up with alien gods by serving and worshiping them, then the guarantee is off: I'll wipe Israel right off the map...

and Israel will become nothing but a bad joke among the peoples of the world... 'Whatever happened here? What's the story behind these ruins?'

Then they'll be told, 'The people who used to live here betrayed their God, the very God who rescued their ancestors from Egypt; they took up with alien gods, worshiping and serving them. That's what's behind this God devastation. (1 Kings 9:6-9)

The culture which enveloped Israel was shaping her into its mould, as daily her knowledge of God and his purposes for his people was deconstructed. The onslaught from Babylon would formidably demolish Israel's faith. It was tempting to now believe that Babylon's pantheon of gods was much more powerful than Yahweh, the God of the covenant.

The second question, *'Have you not heard?'* confronts Israel with another question, 'What are you listening to?'

The prophet is keenly aware that Israel is not putting into practice what she already knew about God. The Hebrew understanding of listening always conveyed the notion of application or obedience. When Jesus says to the crowds, 'He who has ears to hear, let him hear,' he is not merely saying to them: 'Pay attention!' Rather, he is saying, 'If you have got a hold of what I am on about, the evidence will be your willingness to follow me to the end.'

When I say to my son, 'Clean up your room,' I am anticipating that it will be followed by a corresponding action. The evidence that he has heard and understood will be either a clean room or the mess remaining.

Israel had actually closed her ears to God, as she forgot who he is and what he had done throughout her history. With some dashes of humour, even sarcasm, Isaiah portrays Yahweh in a provocative way. The prophet's aim is that Israel might have a clearer and truer focus of who God truly is; who she is in relation to him and how the warping of her faith has caused these wobbly steps. Furthermore,

'So – who is like me? Who holds a candle to me?' says the Holy.

'Look at the night skies: Who do you think made all this?

Who marches this army of stars out each night,

Counts them off, calls each by name – so magnificent! So powerful! – and never overlooks a single one?' (Isaiah 40:25-26)

Here the prophet is seeking to achieve two things: he is drawing Israel's attention away from Babylon and he is trying to remove the scales from her eyes.

In the ancient world, Babylon was the home of astrology, believing that the stars were gods and determined human destiny. Israel was being exhorted to see with new eyes – eyes of faith – and hear with new ears – ears of faith – that the Holy One was entirely responsible for the future of civilisations. With panache, the prophet depicts God as a school principal assembling pupils on the parade ground. So it is that God assembles and calls each star by name – and not one of them is missing! They are where they belong and where he has placed them in his universe.

Because I can say this about the stars, how much more do I value you, O Israel?

It is like Jesus centuries later regarding the common sparrow that falls to the ground and the number of hairs on a person's head. Absolutely nothing goes unnoticed by him...

If Israel can embrace both questions related to 'knowing' and 'hearing', then her exilic experience will grace her with new eyes and new ears to see who God is and who she is. Similarly, *'Do you not know and have you not heard?'* (40:28) will have introduced the prospects of an answer coming.

Israel's sense of lostness about the character of God and his covenant relationship with her will take on an entirely different perspective when seen in this context. And if this were not enough, there is more firepower from the prophet Jeremiah. For he removes any doubt as to 'O God, where the hell are you?'

This is what the Lord God Almighty, the God of Israel says to all those I carried into exile from Jerusalem to Babylon. (Jeremiah 29:4)

Did you catch who it is that is speaking to Israel? It is none other than the God of Israel. 'Where you are is where I want you to be. You are here because I am still the God of Israel. I am undefeated and undaunted by Babylon's bragging rights. Babylon, like every other nation and kingdom of this world, is in my hands, just as you still are.'

Quite significantly, the word exile contains a world of meaning. It is derived from the Hebrew word *gâlâh* – 'to reveal' or 'uncover', which has the connotation of 'to denude,' especially in a disgraceful sense. This is obviously what often occurs for people taken into captivity.

However, this same Hebrew word is one which we would normally associate with revelation.[17] And this is precisely what God has in mind with Israel in exile. Not only will Israel have a new and fresh vision of God but she will see herself for who she really is. Israel is being laid bare and is naked before God, because exile is truly the place of uncovering.

This must not be interpreted only in a punitive and humiliating sense for Israel. It will have special significance far beyond her day and into the world to come because of Jesus...

Thunder in the desert! Prepare for God's arrival...
God's bright glory will shine and everyone will see it.
Yes. Just as God has said. (Isaiah 40:5-6)

For Israel, exile will be an uncovering of the truth of her relationship with God. Therefore all is not lost. 'To you Israel, Babylon appears to be like hell; however, I am right there with you. I carried you there and I shall at the right time bring you home in a breathtakingly amazing way. But first you must return to me, for I am truly your home!

'Your words of exasperation and your deepest groans have not fallen upon deaf ears. As I gave you words of exhortation, so now hear my words of expectation...'

Words of expectation

He gives strength to the weary,
and to him who lacks might he increases power.
Though youths grow weary,
and vigorous young men stumble badly
Yet those who wait for the Lord,
Will gain new strength,
They will mount up with wings like eagles,
They will run and not get tired,
They will walk and not become weary. (Isaiah 40:30-31)

The tables have turned. Can you hear the echo of a previous story in Israel's history with God? 'Just as I carried you out of Egypt on eagles' wings to myself. This word image comes right out of the Exodus account; now, Israel, you are to get ready for what I am about to do with you. Wait for me and wait on me, for it is now your turn. You must fly with your own wings of faith.

'But be patient, Israel. Do not pray to get out of there, or your focus will be exclusively on yourself. Instead, take this opportunity to express your faith in exile. Listen again to my servant the prophet Jeremiah.'

Build houses and make yourselves at home.
Put in gardens and eat what grows in that country.
Marry and have children.
Encourage your children to marry and have children so that you'll thrive in that country and not waste away.
Make yourselves at home there and work for the country's welfare.

Pray for Babylon's well-being.
If things go well for Babylon, things will go well for you." (Jeremiah 29:5-7)

Centuries later, Jeremiah's words resonated with the apostle Paul as he wrote to the Christian community in Rome.

So here's what I want you to do, God helping you: Take your everyday ordinary life – your sleeping, eating, going to work, and walking around life – and place it before God as an offering. Embracing what God does for you is the best thing you can do for him. Don't become so well adjusted to your culture that you fit into it without thinking. Instead fix your attention on God. You'll be changed from the inside out. (Romans 12:1-2)

In other words, God says, just get on with living with me as the centre of your life. Learn to live life loved by me wherever you find yourself. Be 'welfare carriers' and allow others to 'fare well' with you in their midst. Learn to be at home with me as I want to with you!

Pastoral prophets such as Isaiah, Jeremiah, and Paul were very conscious of sustaining the community in their journey of faith. They were able to discern the prevailing godless cultures of Babylon or Rome which sought to suck the life of faith out of believers and wipe out their true identity with the one true God. The intent of these cultures was to cause followers of Jesus to lose their way and be seduced into accommodating other gods.

For Israel, exasperation had caused confusion, grief and a deepening sense of being abandoned and lost by God. And yet the prophets exhorted Israel not to lie down and give in, but to give voice to God. As we choose not to surrender to exasperation and allow ourselves to hear God, we come to a point of expectation. It is true that God is with us in our pain, but he never indulges us in our pity parties.

Even feeble faith, when infused with expectation, begins to see that it is actually God who has carried us here. Babylon, with all its bluster and bravado, is purely an instrument in God's hands for the execution of his will and purpose for Israel. She must hear what God has spoken to her, namely: 'Exile must not exorcise your trust or dependency on me.'

To a community of people living in exile, miles from their home, defeated, their beloved city burned to the ground, their very existence in danger, not even sure who they are any longer, the prophet speaks of God's faithfulness with his people:

Don't be afraid, I've redeemed you.

I've called your name. You're mine.

When you're in over your head, I'll be there with you.

When you're in rough waters, you will not go down.

When you're between a rock and a hard place, it won't be a dead end.

When you walk through fire you shall not be burned...because I am GOD, your personal God, the Holy of Israel, your Saviour.

(Isaiah 43:2, The Message and NIV)

The word pictures evoke very powerful symbols: fire, water, everything that threatens, chaos, destructiveness, death itself; yet through the prophet, God says: 'Don't be afraid, I have called you by name, you are mine'. Despite those things that cloud Israel's judgment of who God is and where she is, God knows her name.

Names are important to God. He knows who we are and whom we belong to. Names tell us that we are known, so we must wait for him and wait on him.

Isaiah's wisdom in waiting

...Yet those who wait for the Lord... (Isaiah 40:31)

The real difficulty we have is with that small word, wait! This is not an easy thing to do. Waiting might seem like a recipe for inactivity, but learning to come to a place of patient rest in God requires a lot of inner action. It means wrestling with our hearts and heads when they are in a state of agitated tumult. Because stillness runs deep, it cannot be achieved overnight.

If we are honest, we find it so much easier to do something, to engage in external action. That way we at least feel that we have some control over the situation, that we are contributing something and getting somewhere. Yet God says to his people both then and now, 'Wait.' For waiting is such an admission of dependency on God. It is amazingly ironic.

Israel received her name through a dogged wrestling bout between Jacob and the angel of God. It was clearly not a night of inactivity. Through the long night, Jacob wrestled and finally appealed to the angel for a blessing. And as we know from the Genesis narrative the unexpected, indeed unwanted blessing came. The angel struck Jacob on the hip and dislocated it so that for the rest of his life he would limp. And then the angel of God conceded to the servant of God:

'Your name is no longer Jacob. From now on it is Israel (God-Wrestler); you've wrestled with God and you've come through.' (Genesis 32:28)

This would be the signature name of the entire Jewish race. You do not have to spend too much time around Jewish people to realize just how much they love to argue and how they savour every opportunity to answer questions with more questions! This has to do with wrestling Jacob, the one who signifies Israel. And yet this very word 'wait' also conveys a strong call to hope or expectancy.

That same Hebrew word for 'wait' employed by Isaiah (40:31) – *qâvâh* – is also used by David the psalm maker. Eugene Peterson aptly captures the force of waiting in his translation of Psalm 40:1: 'I waited and waited and waited for God.' The repetition captures David's intensity and hunger, fuelled and filled with expectancy that God will come through for him.

If we as the church in the 21st century want to celebrate our Judeo-Christian heritage, then faith must not be seen as a passive, inactive quality but as one which engages in regular wrestling matches with God. When put on the mat by God, we learn that the true place of submission is not to give in or give up, but to surrender. We do this not blindly, but knowingly, even though 'only knowing in part,' to the one who is saying to us: 'Do not let go of me; do not let me off the hook; I am here for you and with you. I want to be at home with you'.

Isaiah's insightful irony

When searching out the origins of a word like wait, we soon realize that all language has a specific framework and context. Like Israel, we find ourselves located in the bigger narrative of God's story, yet without always being able to grasp what God is doing. This is why it is so important to allow prophetic voices to be heard, as we have found already.

Both Isaiah and Jeremiah are attuned to the Spirit's speech. Isaiah's exhortation to the exiles to wait is inseparably linked with Jeremiah's message about God's precise timetable.

This is God's word on the subject: 'As soon as Babylon's seventy years are up and not a day before, I'll show up and take care of you as I promised and bring you back home. Yes, when you get serious about finding me and want it more than anything else, I'll make sure you won't be disappointed,' God's decree. (Jeremiah 29:11, 13)

The prophet's words are rich with hope and expectancy. Home is geographical, but also a metaphor of God and Israel being at home with each other once again. However, to translate this into reality Israel must heed God's agenda and timing. Irony continues as we follow Isaiah's closing three-fold progression of thought:

For those who wait for the Lord – *they shall soar, fly*

...Yet those who wait for the Lord,

Will gain new strength,

They will mount up with wings like eagles... (Isaiah 40:31)

The eagle has an amazing capacity to soar and see from very high places. So it is that Israel and all who wait upon God will be empowered to soar and see, experiencing his supernatural enabling. We must also learn that soaring comes with learning how to see what God is doing and saying in specific situations and people's lives. He carries us and so we soar with him, but this can only be true when God is at home with us.

For those who wait for the Lord – *they shall run and not be weary*

He gives strength to the weary,

and to him who lacks might he increases power.

Though youths grow weary,

and vigorous young men stumble badly

Yet those who wait for the Lord,

Will gain new strength. (Isaiah 40:30-31)

It is almost unthinkable when the youth, those whom we thought will never grow tired or weary, stumble and fall! And yet, there are times in all of our lives when our get up and go 'has just got up and gone.' We are worn out, exhausted and just plain weary. We are lost and at a distance from God. However, he has not abandoned us, he is right there with us.

So the prophet Isaiah is saying that the Holy One will empower you to run and not be weary. Waiting will teach you not to allow your weariness to govern your relationship with God. Be prepared to run with him, even when it appears impossible. And finally...

For those who wait for God – *they shall walk and not faint*

They will run and not get tired

They will walk and not become weary.

The irony unfolds for Israel and for us, with prophetic words that defy sound reasoning. The normal order of things would be walking, running and then soaring or flying. It is the ascending, ever upward, ever higher. However, the prophet has reversed the entire process: those who wait for God shall soar, run and walk.

Why does Isaiah say it like this? Could it be that God is much more interested in our day to day walking with him, rather than running and soaring?

Yes, we may love the spectacular and dramatic, but God is interested in the consistent journey of walking with him. That is where our Christianity counts. And that is precisely what this book is all about; staying on the long haul. It is about becoming skilled in the art of not getting lost on the way home, which I understand to mean: learning what it means being at home with God even now.

Is there an answer for: 'O God, where the hell are you?'

Most definitely, the answer is a resounding yes. It is neither half-hearted nor a makeshift answer with a few proof texts propping up the scaffolding. Isaiah's words of exhortation and expectation are richly practical in responding to Israel's exasperation about her exile in Babylon. Combined with Jeremiah's insight about how exile is about getting on with living where God has placed you, provides great encouragement.

As Israel's sense of lostness about God's apparent forgetfulness of his promises is responded to, the prophet challenges her to recover faith in the womb of exile. And this is clearly not the end of the matter.

There is still more to be laid out for Israel and for us, the church

44

in the 21st century, as we face the adventure of our lives in learning to trust God. This trust involves allowing God to be at home in us entirely.

When all else around us assaults our hearts and heads, attempting to convince us that God has abandoned us, we have more to learn from the prophet because there are more answers.

Unforgettable, that's what you are to me...

The prophet draws our attention to a very tragic moment in a person's life, when he or she feels abandoned. Although the wound seems unendurable, it is not impossible to heal. Isaiah deftly discloses the character of God to Israel and to us: God will never forget nor abandon anyone.

Can a mother forget the baby at her breast and have no compassion on the child she has borne? Though she may forget, 'I will not forget you'. See, I have engraved you on the palms of my hands... (Isaiah 49:15-16)

These are perhaps some of the most profoundly poignant words ever written about God: The word 'engraved' is stronger than 'inscribed'[18], and inherent in it is the idea of tattoo. It is not merely the writing of a ballpoint pen. Tattoo artists say that the palm of the hand is one of the hardest places on the body to get a tattoo. In fact, most tattoo artists won't even attempt it, because you use your hands all the time, so they don't heal well and the ink wears off; your hands aren't smooth, so they have to go over it several times; it is seriously painful and engraving remains as a permanent scar... but that is precisely how much God loves us.

God cannot forget, God will not forget – ever – your name. Furthermore the image of being tattooed on God's hands 'is a potent reminder that the covenant God makes with his chosen people is no external, bilateral contract, but a divine promise woven into the very fabric of his being.'[19] And God doesn't change his mind about us.

Remember me...

Do you remember Elie Wiesel at the beginning of this chapter? He confronted us with the menacing picture of God and hell on the same stage. In this real-life setting, losing our way and removing ourselves from anything further to do with God might be seen as totally warranted.

For Wiesel, an ominous stench of death was in the air and faith was stretched beyond breaking point. Hope had long ago taken wings, and the question 'Oh God, where the hell are you?' returns...

'For God's sake, where is God?'

And from within me, I heard a voice answer:

'Where he is?

This is where – hanging here from this gallows.'[20]

Painfully and powerfully, the question, 'O God, where the hell are you?' is answered. The answer to humanity's interminable groaning is on that cross of shame and pain – the gallows. Jesus is there for us.

Like Isaiah, Elie Wiesel is seized by the Spirit of God to see Christ on the gallows. For Calvary represents once and for all the place where God endured hell in Jesus Christ his Son. At that precise place, humanity might know that no son of Adam or daughter of Eve need ever spend an eternity separated from him.

Yes, God dies, but neither death nor evil have the last say. At the cross our names were inscribed into the scarred hands of Jesus the Nazarene. His blood was shed and his life was given so that we might never have to live with the dreadful agony of been lost and forgotten forever.

Earlier there were a lot of priests, for they died and had to be replaced. But Jesus' priesthood is permanent. He's there from now to eternity to save everyone who comes to God through him, always on the job to speak up for them. (Hebrews 7:25)

To the Jewish nation, a people so entrenched in the traditional role of the priesthood, the coming of Jesus brings about radical change. Everything is redefined and reinterpreted. We have now been brought into relationship with someone who is literally 'always on the job to speak up for us.'

Above all the clamour and chaos of our world, Jesus hears us and does for us what only he can do, not only making us more like him but intimately drawing us into being at home with his Father. *'The darkness is on its way out and the True Light is already blazing!'* (1 John 2:8b)

'Jesus sticking up for us' became vitally true for one man, a rank outsider, a nobody with any religious affiliation. He called out, 'Jesus, remember me when you come into your kingdom.' On that same stage where 'God put the wrong on Jesus who never did anything wrong, so we could be put right with God' the thief broke his silence, 'remember me'. (Luke 23:42)

God remembers us. Forgiven and not forgotten...my answers are in his scars. The agonising and often excruciating dilemma, 'O God, where the hell are you?' is answered fully by Jesus.

He leads us unafraid and undaunted to his Father, the God who gives us permission to voice the stuff that we may think he does not want to hear. He allows us to accept the inestimable luxury of been loved into wholeness. Sometimes our walking with God will be two steps forward and three steps back, but we must never be put off. Our divine choreographer will persist in teaching us how to keep in step with his unforced rhythms of grace. This is precisely how we do not get lost along the way with him.

Conclusion

The faith journey we have begun calls us into the freedom that allows God to be God. Yet it also invites us to stay awake to the constancy of his speech and his touch all the way. He never wants us to let him off the hook. Being true to our Jewish roots translates into discovering our true identity in Christ. As Jesus wrestled with God and learned to prevail with him, so God loves it when we are candid and committed to him.

If you have stopped having it out with him, you are giving into the lie that you have no voice. That is how we can so easily lose our way. He who knows the very best and the very worst of us, has heard it all before from every saint and sinner throughout the ages. What he longs for from us is ruthless honesty and vulnerable obedience, regardless, of whether we feel his nearness or absence.

God knows that dark powers collude with hellish hosts to deny us our true identity, but he is resolutely committed to skilling us in the art of not getting lost on the way home. For even hell itself cannot extinguish his presence. We learn so much more to appreciate the light when we discover that God is not absent. He is with us all the way.

On the twenty-eighth of May, 1972, the Duke of Windsor, the uncrowned King Edward VIII, died in Paris. The same evening a television program rehearsed the main events of his life. Extracts from earlier films were shown in which he answered questions about his upbringing, brief reign and abdication. Recalling his boyhood as Prince of Wales, he said:

My Father [King George V] was a strict disciplinarian. Sometimes when I had done something wrong, he would admonish me, saying, 'My dear boy, you must always remember who you are.'[21]

I am convinced that our heavenly Father wants to say the same to us every day: 'My dear child, you must always remember who you are.' Learning who you are makes the world of difference in learning to be at home with God right now, not merely in the future.

Negotiating God's paths and navigating his ways can confront us with our sheer inability to stay the distance with him. What often comes to the surface is the insistent appeal of 'O God, why can't I know everything right now?' Our second chapter probes a little deeper, uncovering our impatience to know all the answers yesterday, but also gleaning insights into the purity of knowing, in contrast to the parody of knowing.

Endnotes

1. Elie Wiesel, *Night* (New York: Bantam Books, 1986) 34, 42
2. Metaphorically and not literally; God is everywhere, but, hell represents our inability to change the sphere of where I find myself away from God. It is I who have chosen to exclude him and shut him out of my life.
3. *Night* (4.206-211)
4. *Night* (1986:10)
5. Klaas A.D. Smelik, (ed.,) *Etty: The Letters and Diaries of Etty Hillesum, 1941-1943,* (Grand Rapids: Eerdmans, 2002) 506
6. Smelik: 2002:640
7. Smelik: 2002:519
8. John McKay, former President of Princeton University, encourages us to embrace this paradox.
9. My own community of interpretation is a theological one therefore I am compelled to read these texts from the perspective of either Judaism or Christianity.
10. Isaiah's sprawling vision of God and God's future; Jeremiah - knocked down but not knocked out; Ezekiel's Valley of the Dry Bones – judgment and hope juxtaposed, Lamentations – Immanuel and His people - and many psalms were all birthed in this period of Israelite history when the people had little reason to hope.
11. Refer to a very insightful article by Walter Brueggemann, *Conversations with Exiles, in The Christian Century,* July 2-9, (1997: 630-632)
12. In our own day one people group are the Ethiopian refugees in Kenya, Somalia and Uganda.
13. Refer to Paul Celan and Martin Buber: *The Poetics of Dialogue and 'The Eclipse of God'* Maurice Friedman Religion & Literature Vol. 29, No. 1 (Spring, 1997), pp. 43-6.
14. Walter Brueggemann, *Cadences of Home: Preaching among exiles* (Louisville, Kentucky: Westminster John Knox Press, 1997), 6.
15. It is this reckless self-disclosure which will surface time and time again through not only the stories of God's ways with his people Israel but also, centuries later through the Nazarene Jesus.
16. Genesis 15 to Abraham, the father of the faith.
17. The same word occurs in the context of the conversation between Samuel the boy with Eli the priest and the Lord God, in 1 Samuel 3:7: 'the word of the Lord had not yet been revealed to him.'
18. Sheldon W. Sorge in *Feasting on the Word: Preaching the Revised Common Lectionary, Year A, Volume 1 – Advent Through Transfiguration,* David L Bartlett and Barbara Brown Taylor, ed., (Louisville, Westminster John Knox Press, 2010) 362.
19. Sheldon W. Sorge, *Feasting on the Word, Year A, Vol. 1,* p. 380
20. Elie Wiesel, *Night* (4.206-211)
21. John Stott, *The Message of Romans, The Bible Speaks Today Series:* Leicester: IVP, 1994), p. 187.

Chapter Two
'O God, Why Can't I Know Everything Right Now?'

God has made us capable of seeing the world in relation to him. And yet again and again we insist on seeing it in terms of its relation to ourselves.

However, once we've started letting go of all our fantasies and all our hopes about getting the world under control, we're on the way to coming to terms with a God who will run away from our hopes of control and understanding; God who is beyond compare. (Archbishop Rowan Williams)[1]

The university had completely refurbished its grounds in the summer, resplendent with fountains and beautifully manicured lawns. All that was needed to complete the beautiful environs was the setting up of walkways where the students could access the buildings. However, there was no design available for these paths.

The construction workers were anxious not only to position the walkways but also see what the design would be, but the president of the university failed to comply with their request. Rather, his response was rather enigmatic: 'These asphalt paths will be permanent. Next year will be the right time to install them.

You shall receive my plans then.' The construction workers were unmistakably peeved but had to wait and see.

When the university year began, the students had to walk on the manicured grass to access their classrooms. Soon well-defined trails were noticeable all over the campus in the large islands of beautiful green lawn, connecting all the buildings.

The president of the university contacted the waiting construction workers and said, 'Now you can go ahead and install the permanent pathways. The design is already there. Simply, fill in all the paths you see before you.'[2] The president knew the design was in place, better than any pre-prepared designs. All the anxiety, demands and frustration could simply be answered by two words: 'Trust me.'

My writing emerges out of the Judeo -Christian tradition, and I started my journey of faith by embracing Jesus' words: 'Come follow me.' At first, following Jesus sounded relatively simple. However the challenge is staying true to following Jesus all the way and not getting lost along the way. Getting lost is not all that hard, primarily because, we always want to have our own way.

When Jesus does not come through immediately and we can't see any clear paths, we tend to devise our own ways. In no time we adopt our own way of taking our life back in control. Jesus therefore gets relegated to the side-lines so that we can sort out the mess that we are in. Compounding the problem is our own warped capacity to always want to know everything right now. This only sets us up for what a five-year-old child told me: 'I'm frusturated'!

Knowing and learning the paths of God is not only an art, but it takes a lifetime and then some. At the start of our faith journey, we expect that God will provide detailed explanations outlining how to get from A to Z. When new challenges confront us, emptying our pockets of faith because we cannot see the way ahead, often we can become annoyed with God. And like the construction workers with the president of the university, we too find ourselves passionately protesting that God has not come through on matters which we consider extremely urgent.

Even though we may have all the facts to work with, nonetheless, we must always be conscious that we do not see all things clearly. 'We are squinting in a fog, peering through a mist.' Our petulant persistence with 'Why I can't know everything right now?' can keep us impaled on the horns of our own stubbornness. We are unable to grasp how very different our relationship with God really is in comparison to the realm of human relationships. God is more than a bigger human. He is God.

And language will always be limited. Therefore, instead of being know-it-alls, we need to keep in step with God, the enigmatic educator, who wants to keep us from getting lost along the way.

Humanness meets human-mess

God alone knows how few people are freed from the boredom of thinking only about themselves. They not only authenticate the humanity of Jesus but they also have discovered the art of not getting lost on the way home with him. Furthermore, these are the kind of people that we need to be spending time with and becoming more like.

Admittedly, getting ourselves to such a place demands the constancy of letting go of our huge egos. Facing our egos is a continuum, especially when it means confronting our capability of making a mess of things, not only with our own lives but also with other people.

I met with a woman recently whose tragic story graphically reminded me of this reality. As a three-year-old child she had a deep wound forced upon her. In the hands of a supposedly holy man and his assistant, she endured shattering experiences which put forgiveness well and truly off the map.

Being there with her and for her is what grace is all about. We are both more broken and more mended than we realise. And this is what makes both rational and emotional sense.

Through her heartfelt sobbing, hope against hope, she stammered out words that had not been heard by anyone else for years. For nearly forty three years she had carried that indescribable burden, while at the same time, attempting to live out her life with God and others. She then gave herself permission to allow Jesus to take the child in his scarred hands, such a moment words cannot describe.

There I was, sitting and listening to what she was saying, attempting to imagine the pain and tension, feeling the conflict between rage and grace, hatred and empathy. In one such moment of reflection I realised that forgiveness is typically not something a person does but something which emerges, often very slowly.

Her brokenness brought her to a place of not only being found by God, but also by herself. Letting go of the memory of such abusive evil behaviour allowed God to begin to build his home within her. God was not absent from her, but the deep indescribable wound had controlled and defined her life. She wanted to always help others and make their path clear and uncluttered on their way to God, while hoping to be welcomed in the hearts of others.

Having heard her story, I see that her heart has been enlarged by healing love, and her head has been enriched with truth that now sets her free into being at home with God and herself. Courage is fear saying its prayers in the face of God.

Every human being needs to get over the fantasy that we are without sin ourselves. As Jesus put it, only if you are without sin may you throw stones at those you judge, but do first have a peep inside yourself. Until we are willing to see ourselves as God sees us, not only as flawed, but also as being formed by his courageous Spirit of wholeness, then we can begin living for the first time.

He stays with us forever.

Without his presence, our humanness remains deeply enmeshed

in human-mess, so we cannot be authentically human.

Therefore, those who are no longer addicted to themselves have understood that authentic humanness can only become the genuine article when human-mess meets true humanness in Jesus. To know ourselves as God truly knows us is the centrepiece of his unending love story with humanity, made and remade in his image and likeness. Similarly, to know God as he wants to be known will always be on his terms so that he can be what he specialises in, namely, being God!

God out of the box

Humanity is waiting for followers of Jesus who feel the strong wind of the Spirit, who sense the heights above them and the abyss below and take a deep breath and live lives abandoned to a life-changing God. When our journey homeward begins to become more and more charged with awe and wonder at his ways and wisdom, we realize that life really does not have to revolve around us. Then the journey will never look anything like we could conceive or formulate, manage or strategize.

God pursues us so that he may personally tutor us in the art of discerning his hand at work in our world. When this becomes our vantage point from which to see, we can begin to grasp just how mind-boggling God is as a constant in our day-to-day living. The constancy of his grace and mercy reminds us that he has not abandoned this world. And if we seek to detain God in a box secured by our own theological, religious or philosophical binding, he will simply break free. Throughout church history, seasons of fresh winds have breathed new life and revived thirsty souls, with lively vistas of God's presence.

Could it be that we need to sacrifice our religious worldview before we can ever really begin to find God?

Enigmatic education

God's longing to surprise us is beyond our wildest guesses and even our best thought-out explanations. This occurs with greater frequency than we realize, and especially when we are not even looking or even thinking about God. God remains resolutely the enigmatic educator.

Director and producer Ron Howard captured this for me in his memorable film Apollo 13. Tension abounds and the pressure pushes NASA aeronautical engineers against the wall with the impending prospects of a failed mission to the moon. Loved ones, family and the entire world are watching the catastrophe unfold before their very eyes on television.

Against this dramatic background, the astronaut Jim Lovell's moment of self-disclosure with a television reporter causes everyone to sit up and listen. When asked, 'Is there a specific instance in an airplane emergency when you can recall fear? his response left me in no doubt about calling God the enigmatic educator.

Uh well, I'll tell ya, I remember this one time – I'm in a Banshee at night in combat conditions, so there's no running lights on the carrier. It was the Shangri-La, and we were in the Sea of Japan and my radar had jammed, and my homing signal was gone... because somebody in Japan was actually using the same frequency. And so it was – it was leading me away from where I was supposed to be.

And I'm lookin' down at a big, black ocean, so I flip on my map light, and then suddenly: zap. Everything shorts out right there in my cockpit. All my instruments are gone. My lights are gone. And I can't even tell now what my altitude is. I know I'm running out of fuel, so I'm thinking about ditching in the ocean. And I, I look down there, and then in the darkness there's this uh, there's this green trail. It's like a long carpet that's just laid out right beneath me. And it was the algae, right? It was that phosphorescent stuff that gets churned up in the wake of a big ship. And it was – it was – it was leading me home. You know? If my cockpit lights hadn't shorted out, there's no way I'd ever been able to see that. So, you never know... what... what events are to transpire to get you home.[3]

Just when we think we 'know' something, it may be a hint that God is working with us, because he wants to alert us to something else he has in mind. Usually it is not what we had not planned or were not even prepared for. How true this was in the ancient story of Jacob the patriarch, who was ambushed by God. (Genesis 28:10-22)

Jacob had thought that he had God confined to heaven. In the best thinking of the day, God was the powerful but the remote King of the Universe, off somewhere in the sky observing things on earth below. This tidy, manageable system asserted that God started everything, and ever since, has left human beings to fend for themselves.

However, that worldview has been challenged and changed. God is not remote but ever-present. This is so evident in Jacob's encounter with God:

The encounter occurs in a place where no one would expect a religious experience. Jacob is a fugitive; he is not searching for God. He has no religious agenda, but he is seeking safety from his brother. Jacob assumed heaven and earth were entirely separate worlds; that God stays in heaven and that he, Jacob, travels alone.

But wonder of wonders, 'there is traffic between heaven and earth.'

The traffic conveys the picture of what God would seek to communicate with every human being, namely, 'I will be with you and keep you wherever you go, in every age and with every person in search of the sacred or for that matter touched by God.'[4]

When we begin to embrace the truth that God really does accept us with all our limitations, all our mistake-making patterns of behaviour, it is actually very liberating. Doing life with God demands a deeper and richer knowing. Jesus reminded his followers, 'I still have many things to tell you, but you cannot handle them now.' (John 16:12)

Timing is everything, even if we think we might be ready for the answer, God knows very differently. This is because he knows us ever so well.

Despite all of the flying hours noted in Jim Lovell's catalogue of experiences, and the many things he had been taught in the aeronautical curriculum, nothing could equip him for that incident in the Sea of Japan. Literally, Lovell was schooled out of darkness into light and brought safely home.

Similarly, Jacob was only one step away from the biggest encounter that he would have with the God who pursued him. Jacob would be educated in the enigmatic ways of God. Life is a learning curve and more importantly, it is coming face-to-face with an ocean of unlearning as well. This is why we must never resign ourselves to the iron-clad notion that our limitations are permanent, or we will be perpetually stunted, small minded and lost to all that God has for us.

When God slaps our face

I met up with a dear friend for coffee recently. She began to relate her journey with me, 'I have just gone through something quite devastating, and I feel as though God has slapped my face.'

Some might consider this expression to be highly offensive about the character of God, yet I am listening, not to interpret but to hear. She is telling it like it is and being honest about her relationship with God, without the mask of religious jargon.

As the conversation continued, I became increasingly aware that the 'slap in the face' had been God's wake-up call for her. My friend has begun to catch a glimpse of what God has wanted to show her for a very long time. And so it was that God had graced her with the gift of new eyes.

She was not only seeing God differently, but also seeing herself differently. She thought that she knew herself quite well, but she began to unravel in the hands of God. He was taking her up on her request from years past, 'God, whatever it takes, make me real...'

As she spoke, truth made its impact and she began to move through her potentially soul-destroying situation with a keener sense that God was in it with her. God had not absconded; he was in it all the way. As we sat and chatted, my mind gravitated towards Jacob wrestling with God.

The aftermath for Jacob is that he would never be the same. After his encounter, he was left with deep insight that would empower him to continue his faith journey with God. I believe that my friend, too, through the 'slap on her face,' received clear revelation in order to see and live differently.

I asked her, 'Did it hurt?' Her response was out of her mouth before I had even finished my question, 'Hurt! – absolutely, of course it did!' But then she asked me, 'How long do you think the pain will last?' I responded, 'Long, if you hold onto your ideas of how it should all work out. But not too long if you keep taking these brave steps in the spirit of letting everything go. For it is only then that you will see more and more of God's "phosphorous trail" in the present darkness, for he will bring you safely home.'

When we are real with God, he reveals to us that when our life is thriving and flourishing, he is present. Ironically, God is ever-present, even when our world is pitch black and chaotic. His presence is not determined by us, but by his longing love to be at home in us right now.

Getting lost from God does not have to last forever. He knows what forever looks like, therefore, stick close to him and you will find his forever company.

Letting go is moving on

There is no doubt in my mind that my friend will experience many more slaps across the face. God has his own immensely personal way of getting through to each of us at the level of what is uniquely true in our relationship with him. Furthermore, our letting go of everything must not be seen as a one-off deal. It will always be a constant.

When we begin to let go, we have begun the journey of a lifetime of change for the better. It is certainly much more painful if we make God pry open our fingers in order to release what we are holding onto, which may be the very thing that keeps us lost from him...

Is it not his anyway? If we are his, doesn't everything belong to him? And is what we are holding onto actually holding us anyway? Eugene Peterson captured the contrast between wisdom and thoughtlessness in the Proverbs:

You'll find wisdom on the lips of a person of insight,

but the short-sighted need a slap in the face. (Proverbs 10:13)

Whether we are naïve, short-sighted or ignorant, in the bigger scheme of things God is more than capable of giving us nudges. Similarly, he is also adept at giving us a slap across the face. This is not in order to humiliate, rather, it is to awaken us out of our inertia. The fundamental difference between genius and stupidity is that genius has its limitations!

Life with God cannot be viewed just as two steps forward and three steps back. Rather, it is like a dance where we are more often on our faces, than flying through the air with the greatest of ease. Our God is the consummate choreographer and he has not enlisted us as mere extras in his daring drama to reveal himself as God to the world. Be surprised, therefore, at what God will orchestrate to bring you home to his Son Jesus, so that you can begin the real journey of living as he had always intended.

This journey is learning to live in the spirit of letting go of everything, especially ourselves, to him. As we do this, others will begin to see God at work in our lives, not merely our attempts at making ourselves perfect by becoming a spiritual Olympiad or enlisting in a religious program of sin management. Rather than becoming smaller and tighter, we become larger and looser, free from the narrowness of judgmentalism. We become so much more spontaneous.

Larger than life, our life in God will bring forth all the exquisite beauty that is uniquely reflected in humanity surrendered to him. Our ears and eyes of faith enable us to grasp what the Hebrew prophets constantly reminded the people of God, that much of their protestation was levelled at the wrong target. Repeatedly their message was:

'This is not your enemy that has brought this about; it has more to do with God and his strange work with you, his people. The one that opposes you is never bigger or greater than God; even though at times everything appears out of proportion to that reality. What remains an absolute is that God is God not just in the acceptable bits of your life, but in everything. From the beginning to the end and all that is in between, God remains true to who he is.'

In every age unvarnished honesty remains the currency of the kingdom of God. When we feel unjustly treated and let down, and start demanding of God, 'I want pure justice,' we don't know what we are really asking for.

If God dispensed pure justice, there is absolutely no way we could cope. We would all end up on our faces begging for mercy. In his economy, mercy is not getting what you do deserve and grace is getting what you don't deserve. So our enigmatic educator invites us to venture further into the paradox of knowing.

The paradox of knowing

Paradox is definitely intended. We must accept that a neat and tidy doctrine of God and his ways will abbreviate our experience of life with him. For God and his word, the root of all knowing is wonder. The awakening stirs in our hearts as we take the time to gaze around us. The star-studded heavens, the broad expanse of ocean and the giant mountains that obscure even the light with their foreboding presence, make us aware that no human language can describe what it is that captures us with such awe and wonder. Awe and wonder will always be an antidote to irresponsible worship and immature discipleship.

They will release us into expansiveness of imagination, freed to be alive to the God who brings us deeper into mystery and devotion to his paths. He has graced us with well-worn paths of faith, which bear the unmistakable imprints of intrepid followers on the long haul. Along with these imprints are interjections – 'Yada, yada, yada – I know, I know I know.'

And regardless of how defiant or obstinate our posture may be, the truth remains: humanity was never created merely for the restrictions of this world's horizons nor a three-score-and-ten lifespan. God is tenacious in sticking with us. He has placed 'a splinter of eternity in our heart.' Inherent in being human is an immeasurable capacity for knowing.

This knowing is predicated on the truth that God brought us into being so that we can reflect his image and nature in this world. The church has been slowly recovering the language of incarnation, not only as a point of celebration at Christmas, but as essential to its mission and vocation in this world. It is his image re-imaged in us through right of relationship with him as God.

This knowing can make an eternal world of difference in the way that we live our lives now before God and others. For it is eternal values which will be brought into view through human lives surrendered to the eternal One. In the coming of Jesus, eternity invaded the temporary. The temporary was never intended to define our existence. If anything, all that is impermanent is given by God to arouse us to the greater vocation of living life unselfishly.

Yada, yada, yada – revelation

This splinter of eternity in our heart was intended to wean us away from our indulgence in the temporary. It is God wanting to scrub us clean from illusion and idealism about ourselves, our world and especially who he is as the eternal being. It is sheer grace that has inscribed eternity in our heart. This energetic all-out grace, stirs us to find pleasure in knowing and being known by him. For God wants to teach us daily that nothing is ever wasted when it comes to knowing him and knowing ourselves.

By his word and his Spirit, God wants to expose every arrogant assumption that we can live our lives on our own terms. And God will relentlessly call us to reject such ignorant notions of our own self-importance. He knows how detrimental it is in our relationship with him and with others.

In learning the art of not getting lost on the way home, we must see that God is more important than we are. And we cannot get all the answers to all our questions right now, nor should we seek them, because God knows that we would not be able to live them.[5] Life is really about accepting our limits, and yet worshiping a God who stands beyond them.

This paradox of our limitations and the limitlessness of God came home to me in the following example of wry Jewish humour. The Jewish rabbis gathered together for a meeting to prove that God doesn't exist. They had had it with God. One after another, they recounted stories of how the Jewish people had been neglected, abused, put down, and even murdered. They remembered the Spanish Inquisition. They remembered the Holocaust. They told one story after another, and finally they concluded, 'There! God doesn't exist. We've proved it by our own history.' Just then, one of them spoke up. 'Excuse me,' he said, 'but we will have to finish this conversation later; it's time for our prayers.'

Prayers will always be the admission of a symbiotic relationship; our helplessness and his wholeness. But the longer we stay in the company of God, the greater will be our realisation that our faith journey is about our capacity to be enlarged in God's story.

Our enlargement frees us to accept that he knows that our 'Yada, yada, yada – I know, I know...' outburst, is us only pretending that we really do know God. We have already made up our minds about what we believe could be the only way at looking at truth. We can't completely conceal who we really are and what we think about God, others and ourselves.

Sadly, much of what we call thinking is just our ego stating what it prefers and resisting what it does not like. This is evident by our slowness to respond to God even when he has been making gracious overtures towards us all our life.

Although we know that God wants his truth to penetrate us and transform our seeing and hearing, we remain resistant to what he wants us to do in his world. This posture of resistance aborts any attempt of God to bring further revelation to our darkened hearts and minds. Nonetheless, God waits patiently for us to come to a place of non-resistance and non-defensiveness.

Know-it-alls assume that their point of view is the only way that anyone can view the point which they are presenting. But God educates us by making sure that several things will come our way that we cannot handle on our own. And because God is sheer grace, he will remain true to his investment with humanity. He will not leave us dangling on any suspension bridge of our own design because we find ourselves unwilling to cross over to the other side and meet with him on his terms.

God knows how quickly we steel ourselves against him, often because of ignorance or fear in our minds. Yet our resistance of new things shows suspicion, not necessarily courage, and forfeits God's revelation. The true act of courage is to yield to him. For God is intent on leading us into the greater reality of true knowing. As we explore this new path we will embrace a new perspective and uncover a new person, namely ourselves with God.

God's ways with each of us are truly personalised, rather than the stereotyped approach we might assume. He does not process us as if we were commodities on a religious assembly conveyor belt. It's okay for our faith to be informed by our denominational outlook, but it does not mean that God will always do things which will conform to that specific perspective. God is far bigger than any denomination.

All who would venture out on this very human journey of faith must trust God no matter how dark the night or long the day. Let's face the facts: often our prejudiced assumptions affect our interpretation about how God should work. Indeed, there is nothing new under the sun...

But it wasn't long before they forgot the whole thing,
wouldn't wait to be told what to do.
They only cared about pleasing themselves in that desert,
provoked God with their insistent demands.
He gave them exactly what they asked for –
But along with it they got an empty heart. (Psalm 106: 14-15)

Israel's insistent demands gave them exactly what they asked for and more besides – an empty heart. God knows all about the welter of voices which entice us to work everything out all by ourselves without any reference to him. But thank God that his word provides us with moving pictures of how he does come to us, as he came to his people in days past.

God will always be true to his word and his character. We cannot make him into a genie, where the roles are reversed: we are the master and God is our servant. In a world madly chasing after images which are a parody of the reality, God is like no other.

He has always wanted to make himself known to us. And yet because we are often too busy being the centre of the universe and the star in our very own drama, we keep missing God's cues along the way. However, everything is connected, from the most intricate to the most sublime. God made us for relationship.

Relationship

Curiously, this word cannot be found in the entire Bible. Yet its presence is on every page. Characters and communities are ablaze with relationship, be it with one another, or dynamically in relation to the overarching presence of God. The stories in the Scriptures set alight the message that God will never give up on relationship with us in this world or the next.

Relationship is the primary context for God to get to know us. After all, God is after us from the inside out, for the state of the heart is the real art of being human. This is precisely where God wants to set up his home in us.

If we wanted to make headway with someone in a relationship, we either go all out for it, or we convince ourselves that it is much too difficult, right?

If we take it to another level, namely with God, perspective is sharpened. If anything is to transform and transcend my banal, pedestrian way of life, it is a relationship with God. God is enthralled with helping us to become more and more the unique people we were meant to be.

We were imaged from the beginning in the Genesis narrative, and re-imaged through redemptive grace at work in Jesus' death and resurrection by the gift of his indwelling Spirit in our lives. We reflect the glory and likeness of Jesus, clothed in our humanity that is our true identity. No one can take that away from us.

And God is unwavering with humanity. God has made his purposes clear. He has comprehensively invaded this world in and through Jesus' living, dying and rising again. What was once mysterious has now emerged into daylight, and the purposes of God which existed before the foundation of the world are now discernible. Discernible that is, to all who have eyes to see and ears to hear Jesus.

The opening of our eyes and ears must never be understood as a one-off event; it is a continuum. As we continue on the seeing and hearing learning curve which is all about obedience to him, this will keep us from getting lost on the way as we choose to let God be at home in us and with us.

Beginning with Jesus is only the first step. Undeniably it is the most decisive step in a journey of many steps with him in our life. For this very reason, the reality of knowing begins and ends with Jesus, for he alone can make sense of the paradox of who God is. Just as there is a paradox in knowing God, there is also a parody of knowing…and this is played out in the garden setting of Eden with two people whose eyes were opened.

The parody of knowing

Parody is an imitation or caricature of the real and the genuine knowing born out of an intimate relationship with God. This parody of knowing represents that which is unwelcoming to the reality of knowing. However, reflect for a moment on David's prayer and a Proverb which is a well-known favourite for all who would learn to navigate the paths of God:

Show me how you work, God;
School me in your ways. (Psalm 25:4)

Trust the Lord with all your heart

Lean not on your own understanding.
In all your ways acknowledge him
And he shall direct your paths. (Proverbs 3:6)

A cursory glance at both passages indicates that they have everything to do with knowing the ways and wisdom of God. Their appeal to us is that they offer traction to stay on the path as we try to make sense of God and his ways. Furthermore, we can also be supremely confident that God responds to them. But what is significant in the art of not getting lost on the way home is one word which ties these verses together.

In Hebrew, the word used for 'show' and 'acknowledge' derives from the same origin, namely, yâda' – 'know'. Etymologically, this 'knowing' encompasses a great variety of perception, euphemistically, figuratively, literally or inferentially. Yâda' expresses much more than mere recognition. It far transcends downloading data from the text book called the Bible and mentally sorting its contents. Rather, it carries within it the sense of intimacy and self-disclosure.

Therefore, yâda' from both Psalm 25:4 and Proverbs 3:6 refers to a level of knowing which exceeds the cognitive and engages us at a far deeper level. Our minds matter to God, but we must be even more attentive to engage fully in what is being presented.

However, parody will keep us impaled on the obvious rather than pushing us beyond, into places where we may not choose to go. The journey of faith is a spiritual reality which cannot be achieved simply by academic erudition. Faith engages with truth, but truth is far more than propositions, creeds or confessions. These all have their proper place, however they have their limitations in their attempt to articulate what is essentially unknowable, especially when it comes to God.

For faith to be faith in the Christian journey, our knowing must be born out of a relationship with God and ourselves. The reality of this knowing conveys more of a communion, a meeting and coming together of persons rather than the mere acquisition of information. The fact that a relationship exists underscores the reality which we have been brought into. It is all of God.

He initiated it, and as C S Lewis describes his own encounter with Jesus: 'I was brought into it kicking and screaming, nevertheless, born into it.' This is why our garden rendezvous with the first humans carries such great significance. As we seek to discern what they were grappling with regarding this knowing born out of relationship, we shall begin to see that the way ahead is fraught with many surprises.

The garden rendezvous

When this word 'yâda [at least a derivative of it] is first used in the Hebrew Scriptures, it is surrounded by an air of unease. In the first chapter of Genesis there is a conspicuous absence of any prohibitions, there are simply commands. However, as the narrative continues, it is not too long before we are struck for the first time with a prohibition on man.[6]

...you must not eat of the tree of knowledge of good and evil, for as soon as you eat of it, you shall die. (Genesis 2:17)

The first humans are specifically forbidden to access knowledge which God alone truly knows. To possess all that God knows would conjure up the idea not only of distancing ourselves from a relationship with him, but also, seeing ourselves as having no need of God. Our creed could be the closing lines of Invictus: 'I am the master of my fate: I am the captain of my soul'.[7]

Tragically, this is precisely the script that has been played out through the centuries with the sons of Adam and the daughters of Eve. Ruthlessly, the serpent works away with humans to engender a mind-set predisposed to wanting to know all, without reference to the all-knowing one, namely, God.

The serpent's strategy is to always create distance from God so that truth about our relationship with him is dissected. For the serpent knows only too well the great attraction that we humans have in wanting to be know-it-alls. In effect, the serpent in orchestrating this drama is saying to the first humans:

'You can go onto bigger and better things, and you must not miss out on anything. You do not need anyone to tell you anything different, take my word for it. For I know how much better things should be and can be. That way, you can live your life grooming yourself in the glory of self-sufficiency. Yes, why shouldn't you know everything?'

In the garden what is on offer to the woman from the serpent is the inestimable luxury of 'knowledge'... 'just like God knowing everything.' We ask ourselves, 'What will she do with the offer? And how will she respond?' The serpent lingers and enticingly whispers...

'Do I understand that God told you not to eat from any tree in the garden?...God knows that the moment you eat from that tree, you'll see what's really going on. You'll be just like God knowing everything, ranging all the way from good to evil.' When the woman saw that the tree looked like good eating and realized what she would get out of it – she'd know everything! – she took and ate the fruit and then gave some to her husband, and he ate. Immediately the two of them did 'see what's really going on' – saw themselves naked! ...they hid from the Lord God. And the Lord God called them. (Genesis 3:1, 4-8)

Alarmingly, this knowing would not just be any knowledge. If we can just begin to grasp the correspondence between knowledge and power, than we may catch a glimpse of what the serpent was on about. In medical science, the moment a new discovery is made in a specific field of research, it is named. The name attached implies power, power accorded to the one whose name the new finding represents. Naming means power over the very thing named.

The serpent was fully alert to the potential of what knowing would do for the woman, Adam and of course, all humanity. In his words, 'it would make them like God, knowing everything.' With cunning guile the serpent has got her intoxicated with the addictive surge of potentially 'seeing what's really going on.' Paradoxically however, humanity must discover the truth that we see only in part...

Faith does invite us to explore with God the paths he would have us to walk on, but it is for the primary reason that we can be empowered to live as he intended. For as we learn to see, so we learn to live life as God intended. As we learn to live 'knowing only in part,' it is the partial that keeps us humble, patient, non-judgmental and alert to being known, not merely a 'know-it-all.'

In the conversation between the serpent and the woman, the word 'God' still hangs in the air. For the serpent knows that he must not give any hint that he is actually stealing her away from God. In his guile he knows that isolation will spawn fantasy, diminishing humanity's capacity for reality.

The chance to know something new may actually cloud what is already true. This does not nullify our quest for the new; the quest for truth is undone only in exchange for truth that keeps us as the centre of attention.

Centuries later, this strategy of isolation would expose the serpent and in effect bring about its demise. It is not a garden but a wilderness, where the serpent would be stripped of his guise by Jesus. Even though Jesus was isolated from his followers, nonetheless he was in the company of the Holy Spirit. Jesus would unveil the parody purveyor as 'the father of lies.'

What we notice in this garden rendezvous is the great dexterity of the serpent in concealing his hand. He wants to make stick the brooding notion that God is ungenerous:

'Do I understand that God told you not to eat from any tree in the garden?'

'Is God trying to withhold things from you and keep them to himself?'

'Do you need God at all any more?'

'Why shouldn't you know all things for yourself right now?'

The fatal attraction

As the story unfolds, the narrator describes the serpent as 'clever' 'ârûm (Genesis 3:1). This Hebrew word carries a fascinating connection with the word 'naked' 'ârôm (Genesis 2:25). Cleverness denotes one's ability to get inside something and uncover more than the obvious. The subtlety of the serpent's craft is clearly to seduce Eve with the delectable thought of being ravished and empowered with knowledge – and his strategy has not changed.

The serpent went all-out to undress her understanding of truth, so that he could begin to dress up her mind with fanciful notions of what she was really missing out on. And of course, the undressing was with sleight of hand and shrewd design, and just to push the blade in deeper, on the pretext that God was actually keeping all this from her.

'Allow me to whisper in your ear: God certainly wants you to think for yourself and the time is at hand. Let yourself embrace what is really yours. You will enjoy the pleasure of standing on your own two feet. Just think how wise and discerning you will become. You have sensed the pleasure in the fruit of knowing. Its arousal to stir you has made you want to go after that which you have never experienced before.'

'See, come, take and eat, and be wise', says the serpent. Infectiously, the serpent continues to tease and tantalize with more morsels of truth. However, it is truth marinated with toxic consequences.

The woman said to the serpent, 'We can eat from the trees in the garden. It's only about the tree in the middle of the garden that God said, "Don't eat from it, don't even touch it or you'll die."' The serpent said to the woman, 'You won't die...' (Genesis 3:2-4a)

Distortion is already evident, as Eve adds her extra – 'don't touch' and the serpent consistent with his nature as a liar, 'you won't die.' The conversation is designed to direct her along a new path of knowing uninhibited by consequences, accountability or responsibility. This scene recalls Eve's gluttonous indulgence in Milton's Paradise Lost where she first eats the apple:

for Eve
Intent now wholly on her taste, naught else
Regarded, such delight till then, as seem'd
In fruit she never tasted, whether true
Or fancied so, through expectation high
Of knowledge, nor was God-head from her thought,
Greedily she ingorged without restraint,
And knew not eating Death.[8]

The clever serpent, intent on enslaving humanity, continues ever-vigilant in keeping them from the reality of knowing which would avert the impending crisis in the garden. The reality is that God in his utter goodness would right the wrong of the serpent and reveal the redemptive plan for humanity through his Son Jesus. This of course would come in due time.

The knowledge of death was also mediated by God to prepare, not to terminate, his children. It was a revelation about their relationship with him as the Lord God, and of the disastrous consequences of exchanging the truth for a lie. These consequences would have bearing on God and all humanity, as well as the serpent, representing all who are predisposed to parody, not reality.

The serpent is diametrically opposed to transparency and his primary ploy is to control his captives. There are no boundaries or lines of demarcation when it comes to this 'knowing' and no clue of the consequences must ever be given to his vulnerable victim. If the fatal attraction of 'knowledge' is to succeed, it must transcend mere physicality and titillation. The serpent is much too brazen and clever not to know that.

The serpent lulls Eve along a path which is entirely new for her, but designed to bind her to herself, without thought of God. Intoxicated and enticed, unaware and unknowing, she will be the main course in a feast of magnificent proportions: 'Knowing like God...'

Who could resist such an invitation, free to feast on the fetish of knowledge?

The wound of knowledge

Conspicuously silent, Adam is irresponsible by his isolation and inactivity. By submitting themselves to the acquisition of knowledge, in direct violation of what God had intended, both have been deeply wounded. Neither cosmetic surgery nor religious makeover can repair the wound. Not even sewing fig-leaves together as makeshift clothes can hide the depth of that wound. And this of course is the ultimate parody of knowledge:

A knowing that binds, but does not bless

A knowing that wounds rather than heals

A knowing that covers over and is not prepared to uncover

A knowing that entraps and does not enlarge.

Desire for knowing has created an incision through many layers of skin. Their fatal attraction to gaining knowledge without a relationship with God leaves them fraught with ambivalence. They had seen before, but never anything like what they are now seeing.

They are stuttering and stammering with their words in order to squeeze themselves out of their uncomfortable predicament. How terribly wrong it all appears. But their eyes are wide open. What was free and fluid in their conversation with God and each other has now changed entirely. The atmosphere is isolation and estrangement, with the spectre of unease filling the air. Lostness prevails...

Imagine what it would have been like for Adam and Eve to be in the company of God at the end of that day, when he walked and talked with them in the Garden of Eden? In those visits, the one that embodies all that is truth would administer reality like an intravenous drip. This would be a daily dosage of reality, not just information, because this was not like a conference but a communion.

Unlike a scrutiny of ID cards visibly displayed in a prominent place, meeting with God would encapsulate disclosure of unravelling proportions. God meets with us primarily, not merely to inform or instruct, but in order to form us from the inside out. This is because he wants so much for us to be with him. This is the essence of not getting lost on the way home, for our home is God.

Creation's unparalleled skies, unprecedented colours and unsurpassed designs all combine to show off the artistry of the great artist, God, before these wide-eyed and open-eared humans. And if the sublime were not enough, Creator God himself was ever present, not lurking with club in hand in readiness to punish, but rather to disclose his voice and presence with them.

And on this specific day, eyes were opened. It is not that eyes were not opened before. However, on this occasion, I have often wondered whether their seeing would be like the man whom Jesus encountered, whose seeing was 'men as trees walking.' He required a second touch from Jesus.

For the careless couple, opacity and not clarity of vision was the outcome. Togetherness would be exchanged for trauma and terror in their relationships with the world around them, the world within them and the world of God. The serpent in the Garden had dangled truth playfully, yet perversely before Eve. Against the dark backcloth of their depravity from which they could no longer protect themselves, Eve and Adam would have realised that they couldn't handle the truth. This fact would have underscored the reality which God alone knew that his children were unable to cope with.

In our own times, disenchantment with political, economic and religious leaders is valid, and the call for accountability is a must. Postmodernism makes its vociferous demand for the real and the genuine. However, ideas related to the real and the genuine must always throw us back onto the all-absorbing issue of God. God is not just in touch with reality; rather he is the singular reference point for reality.

And this is precisely where followers of Jesus factor into the scenario. People in relationship with Christ always have been God's show-and-tell visual aid before a watching and desperate world. And this is precisely why reality came into this world embodied in the humanity of Jesus the Nazarene.

Truth can only find its definition when it is born out of relationship with the one who is truth, namely Jesus Christ. Jesus showed his followers a way to live, organically connected with truth, which empowers a person to celebrate the life which God had intended from the very beginning (John 14:6). In Jesus, everything that is real and true regarding humanity at home in God finds genuine expression.

Reality and truth can only come alive in human beings when daily surrender to Jesus is a lifestyle, not a form of legalism or perfectionism, or an escape route from this world to secure a reservation in the next. And so the unveiling of the way, the truth and the life continues in this world through the presence of God inhabiting and empowering all who are in Christ.

Therefore the wound of knowing inherited through our first parents must undergo invasive healing at the deepest level of our human-mess. Authentic humanness can only be found as God takes up residence in people who allow him unhindered access to every aspect of their life.

Uncomfortable knowing...

The serpent is not heard from again in the garden, but his work to deceive and darken the minds of Adam and Eve has been accomplished. Unopposed by the now condemned serpent, the Lord God speaks to his children. He comes to them, just as he had with the animal parade before Adam (Genesis 2:19-20). God's availability to them is a given. His vibrant presence moves among them, as he has walked and talked with them before in the garden (Genesis 3:8). He has listened to his children even before they have spoken to him.

Once my brother and I were keenly aware that we had done something very bad. Quite clearly it was altogether wrong, there was no one else to blame. We sat nervously, rehearsing the lines of our script to distract us from the thought of punishment, although no amount of cover-up would dissuade our father from thrashing us for the shame we had brought on the family.

In the garden, the man and the woman were caught out, despite their scapegoating of each other. Their new knowledge of good and evil has already made its detrimental impact upon their lives. Even before they get caught, they are caught out by their own guilt and shame, as their new knowledge, rather than introducing freedom, has generated fear. They were left uncomfortable and alone with each other. Indeed, 'knowledge' was at the heart of the fall. Could this be death itself, predisposing their heads and hearts to the deepening futility of being utterly alone forever?

In the garden, perhaps we hear Adam and Eve conversing...

'I did hear him say quite explicitly, "You won't die." Did we not together share in this and assume that there would not be any repercussions? How is it that this new knowing has rendered us powerless?'

'We are manacled to the grip of impotency. We are left isolated and noxious to one another and, worst of all to ourselves. Life and death have made their presence known in the starkest of terms.'

'I know, but somehow I do not know. If anything, all that relates to my way of seeing has become distorted. I am at a loss in this relationship because it is an uncomfortable knowing. Is this how it should be? Adam, I am not seeing too well at all...'

If a picture paints a thousand words

As the narrator moves us forward, we find ourselves arrested by a scene throbbing with high emotion. The first two humans awkwardly prepare to meet God...He comes 'in the cool of the day,' in direct contrast to Adam and Eve who are burning up with the agitation of fear and shame. They learned to be afraid the wrong way.

So they set in motion for the entire world the search for scapegoats, someone or something to blame. Why bother owning up and taking responsibility, there is always someone else who can pick up the tab?

However, there is a way of learning things properly. The steep learning curve demands nothing other than vulnerability, transparency and responsibility. When these are our true companions, we celebrate truth that forms us and frees us into being at home in God. Adam and Eve's response to God reveals the distance that has been created, rendering them neither remorseful nor taking responsibility for their act of betrayal.

By the end of the third chapter of Genesis, the parody purveyor

– the serpent – has spawned his offspring, namely, excuses. The conspicuous evidence of this is found upon the lips of the guilty couple (Genesis 3:12-13). Undeterred, God wants them both to know that he doesn't forgive the excusable; rather he specializes in forgiving the inexcusable.

Only when our eyes are truly opened by God, can we begin to catch the cascading light from the face of the one who knows the best and the worst of us, it is love. No amount of running and hiding can ever produce enough excuses. Listen to one who has drunk deeply from the reality of this knowing:

'I find that when I am asking God to forgive me I am often in reality (unless I watch myself very carefully) asking him to do something quite different. I am asking him not to forgive me but to excuse me. But there is all the difference in the world between forgiving and excusing… If one was not really to blame then there is nothing to forgive.'

'In that sense forgiveness and excusing are almost opposites… we shall go away imagining that we have repented and been forgiven when all that has really happened is that we have satisfied ourselves with our own excuses. They may be very bad excuses; we are all too easily satisfied about ourselves…All the real excusing God will do. What we have got to take to him is the inexcusable bit, the sin.'[9]

The all-knowing God, who speaks and acts in order to commune with his children, comes. He knows that they know that he knows. God knows that they have acquired knowledge through the malevolence of the beguiling serpent. Something new and strange has transpired between God and his children.

Just as their eyes have been opened, so now their senses have been made alive to an uncomfortable intimacy, the like which they have not known. Not only does God call to Adam, 'Where are you?' but he also touches them both.

The timing is quite startling. It is after their act of rebellion. We need to capture the intended poignancy.

'The Lord God made garments of skins for Adam and his wife, and clothed them,' (Genesis 3:21, NIV). At this moment there is reciprocity of knowing between God and Adam and Eve. Adam has shared their new-found knowledge: *'We are naked and ashamed and we hid in the trees and hid from [you] God'.*

They do see and they do know. God knows just how deep this wound of knowledge is within them, and he knows that they can never be the same again. As representatives of all humanity, this wound of knowledge would form a deep artery in the human soul through which all manner of good and evil would flow.

Furthermore, their miscalculation about what they would gain by way of possession of knowledge, now translates into powerlessness. The two have become one, but not as God had intended. Isolation has malformed intimacy, so that their oneness is a mirroring of their helplessness and shame. Guilt of this magnitude will always find an accomplice.

Though some have interpreted this unsettling scene where Adam and Eve are expelled from the beautiful environs of the garden as vindictiveness, look again. As if God's calling out to them were not enough, like a tailor he fashions their garments and clothes them. The growing tension escorts us further into the depths of God's character.

The serpent enticed the woman and the man into the path of knowing, only to strip their understanding of God and leave them in tatters. Now however, it is God who dresses their true nakedness with pure knowing, graced through relationship with him. God comes for them when they are embroiled in shame. He envelops his children with the shelter of his own presence. He comes not to scold, for they have successfully done this to themselves. They are soiled.

Far from their new knowledge bringing security, it has brought censure. However, God's parting gesture is not to throw them out, isolated and stranded; he knows they are helpless and vulnerable in an entirely new world.

Parody versus Reality

What they had assumed would bring power has only brought a perversion of power. And this is sin. It seeks to fulfil legitimate needs illegitimately. It is not desire in itself which is wrong; but rather, it is the knowledge of one's desire which generates shame. Adam's exultant reaction on first seeing the woman certainly implies that he had desired her from the start. Then: *'the two were naked...yet unashamed.'* (Genesis 2:25)

When their eyes were opened, desire became understood desire, admitted need, which shames. Their wounds are open and must be covered. Provision is made for them, not merely for their healing, but also that they may be helped in understanding who God is and how he deals with sin. Reality demands a greater price; parody always gives in to the imitation.

The Lord God does not leave a promissory note reassuring and directing them to a clothing bin at the end of the garden. Rather, he himself puts these garments on them. As he comes to mediate on their behalf, he wants Adam and Eve to never forget who he is and what they mean to him. It is altogether true that God wanted humanity to reflect his image, but also he wanted their company. In direct contrast, the parody of knowledge on offer from the serpent would only ever bring:

Dissonance, not resonance

Discord, not accord

Toxicity, not transparency

Enslavement, not empowerment

Self-interest rather than interest in God and others.

Over the years, it is with great sadness and anger that I have met people whose appetite for Biblical and theological knowledge has not changed them into vitally warm and loving human beings. If anything, they flaunt their knowledge in order to overtly and covertly manipulate the lives of people entrusted to them by God. Having perfected the art of appearing spiritual – adept at polished clichés and attractive performances – they have abandoned their first love, neither ministry, nor church leadership, but Jesus.

Not only have I been found in their company, but I am sure that this is the strategy of the evil one. This parody of knowledge is accessible to anyone – Christian or non-Christian – but it comes with a severe price tag, the willingness to be defiantly duplicitous in public and in private life. And this describes people who have lost their way with God. God is clearly not at home with them.

The light is on, God is not absent. It is just that they are choosing to make themselves more present in what they are doing for God rather than actually being intimate with God. This parody of knowing is seen at its worst in religion. For parody without purity can simply skill us in producing a deceptive 'religion' which evades the reality of the relationship that God really wants with us. Parody negates any possibility of incarnational living as Jesus modelled to us. When I alone must have centre stage, there can be no room for another.

Were their eyes opened to the truth? Yes and no! Eyes were opened, yet only partially. They were unwilling to allow the penetrating Spirit of God to open their eyes even further to the truth about themselves and what God wanted to be to them and with them as people whom he could entrust with others. They were not to be merely dispensers of biblical or theological information, but rather to be Jesus in his world.

David captures the spirit of this seeing and knowing in the language of on-going transformation:

God rewrote the text of my life
When I opened up the book of my heart to his eyes. (Psalm 18:24)

Eyes wide open

The opening of our eyes is but the beginning of our never-ending story. Some of us have begun this journey with Jesus at some time past, but have stalled along the way and allowed ourselves to be lost to everything else but God. We can be so lost in the myriad of programs of serving in church that we become out of touch with God. In the tyranny of the career and vocational identity we can be lost to our authentic identity in Christ. The litany of lostness goes on and on; simply fill in the blank what applies to you in your specific arena.

We are so like our first parents in the garden, adept at hide and seek, all the while insulting the Spirit of grace. In our cowardly bravado we are unwilling to be honest with Jesus about our life of distortion. My personal experience has repeatedly been that when humility is prized, it ushers in healing. With light breaking in, our eyes and ears are being opened to Spirit speech. God has come and made himself utterly vulnerable, enfolded in death on the cross.

His dying and death reaches me: 'Van, I am naked and ashamed; this is for you. Accept what I offer; it is entirely and unreservedly free; allow me to be dressed up in your skin, in and for this world.'

This is a beautiful exchange indeed. It is beginning to see, even though partially, walking naked and unashamed in his company; being with the one who wants to be at home with me in his unending story. It is being alerted to seeing him, the one who is love, and who continues to love. He is the one who will always teach me how to love like he loves.

This is the vision of the God whom I carry within my heart. It sustains me for the long haul, even though I know full well, that as I walk with God, my own stupidity and recurring unwillingness to say what I mean and mean what I say can cancel out this intimacy of relationship with him.

Because basically, I find that I am no different to others who are warlike, greedy, racist, selfish, and vain, and still believe that Jesus is their 'personal Lord and Saviour.' However, the world has no time for such silliness anymore. The suffering on Earth is much too great.[10]

Even when our eyes have been opened, the parody purveyor will do his utmost to distract and distort our perception of the true paths to walk in, so that we will get lost on our way to being at home with God. The serpent still has deceptive designs in mind. His strategies are masterful and entirely malicious in preparing us for our demise.

Adam and Eve did obtain knowledge but it was not the knowledge they needed. If they were to assume responsibility for this knowledge they needed to know both themselves and God. The acquisition of this double knowledge for them and for us can only become ours through the full-bodied appropriation of truth.

Truth worth knowing impacts the intellect, yet it can never be contained by it or be a subject of research so that we may construct an essay on the attributes of God. Rather, this truth is intended to expose the parody in our acquisition of knowledge.

Our relationship with God is meant to evoke celebration of life. When this celebratory note resonates deep in our hearts, we can have increasing confidence that we are experiencing a purity of knowing. It is a knowing born out of relationship with him who alone is genuine truth. Jesus will always place us fairly and squarely on the well-worn path of the reality of knowing.

Conclusion

In grasping hold of an answer to 'Oh God, why can't I know everything right now?' we can readily see that there is so much more at stake than the mere acquisition of knowledge. Our first parents, Adam and Eve, were arrested by their own impotent understanding of God. Their appetite had effectively lured them away from him who is the all-knowing one.

This all knowing of God is always subject to his all-pervasive wisdom and scrutiny. And as the enigmatic educator, not only is he not impatient with us, but he will employ paradox and irony, wonder and awe in order to enlarge our capacity to learn his ways. Lord, lead me out of my small mindedness, into the broader expanse of being honest and humble, as I allow myself to get lost in the vastness of you, my true home!

The paradox of knowing remains a constant. From every angle, the deceiver will always be nibbling at our ears, presenting images and texts before our eyes, enticing us to move away from the reality of all that God chooses to allow us in knowing him. The parody purveyor will persist in peddling his malignant messages of partial truth. It is always partial, because serpent speech invites irresponsibility and non-accountability, with no consequences involved.

In cultivating pure knowing, we may at times find ourselves taking a different route to what we had expected or even planned. But we must not be discouraged by our own inability to understand everything. In learning to ride a bike, we have to be prepared to fall off to eventually learn what balance feels like. Yet those of us who have never allowed ourselves to fall are actually off balance, while not realizing it at all. Could this be the very reason why we are so hard to live with?

As we continue to pursue this reality of knowing, chapter three invites us into a very personal journey with a man who has carried a burning question for a very long time, 'O God, what are you trying to tell me?'

Endnotes

1. The Archbishop of Canterbury preached at an Advent Carol Service at St Martin-in-the-Fields in Trafalgar, 2711/11.

2. John Medina, *Brain Rules: 12 Principles for Surviving and Thriving at Work, Home and School* (Seattle: Pear Press, 2008) 111-112.

3. *Apollo 13*, 1995 film, written by William Broyles Jr. and Al Reinert, based on the book Lost Moon by Jim Lovell and Jeffrey Kluger.

4. Walter Brueggemann, *Genesis: Interpretation: A Bible Commentary*, (Atlanta, GA: John Knox Press, 1982) pp. 242–244

5. See Eugene Peterson, in the author's introduction to Ecclesiastes, The Message (Colorado Springs: NavPress, 2002) 1162

6. Similarly, in the first account of creation 'everything is good' but in the second account 'it is not good that man should be alone' (Genesis 2:18).

7. Quiller-Couch, Arthur Thomas (ed.) (1902). *The Oxford Book of English Verse, 1250–1900* (1st (6th impression) ed.). Oxford: Clarendon Press; Invictus – William Henley, p. 1019

8. R. Bradford, *Paradise Lost* (1 ed.), Philadelphia: Open University Press, 1992, (IX, 785-92)

9. C. S. Lewis, "On Forgiveness" (1947), in *The Weight of Glory and Other Addresses* (New York: HarperCollins, 2001), 178-180.

10. Adapted from CAC Foundation Daily Meditations: Compassionate Action (CD, DVD, MP3), 27/8/2011

Chapter Three
'O God, What Are You Trying To Tell Me?'

'...the greater the truth, the more time one's eyes need
to adjust, to be able to see it.'
(George Hunsinger)[1]

For a number of years I worked within the Central Business District of Brisbane. Often during my lunch break I would slip away without telling anyone and go and sit in the Cathedral of St Stephen. It was within walking distance of my workplace. The space and the quiet, the late nineteenth-century architecture, the icons with their brooding silence and stares, and even the cavernous open door into the cathedral, all served their purpose in directing my thoughts away from myself.

Even though this was but a temporary respite, it was sublime. No liturgy was offered; no priest or curate gave a homily; it was simply being there. This occurred during what I would call my BC days – 'Before Christ.' I labelled these days as such because I had made no conscious effort to follow Jesus or be involved with church life.

Why I frequented the cathedral, I really did not know. So the opening quotation, 'the greater the truth, the more time one's eyes need to adjust to be able to see it,' made profound sense to me much later in my life. And learning to see, or at least, to begin to see has been a very painful journey. The greater truth has impacted me in a number of ways, primarily to expose the 'relentless smell of self in everything about my life.' And yet the image of the 'open door' into the cathedral stayed with me for a very long time and has had a major bearing on my life.

Since I have recovered the places of silence in my life with God, I now see that God has always been my open door. I am welcomed through the open door to greater truth than I could ever imagine, which far surpasses watertight doctrines and creedal confessions. It is truth embodied in the person of Jesus Christ. Because it is only Jesus who puts you and me...

...in touch with everything there is to know of God. Then it is that we will have minds confident and at rest, focused on Christ, God's great mystery. All the richest treasures of wisdom and knowledge are embedded in that mystery and nowhere else. And we've been shown the mystery. I'm telling you this because I don't want anyone leading you off on some wild-goose chase, after other so-called mysteries, or 'the Secret.' (Colossians 2:2-4)

Grace yourself with the gift of taking the time to taste this truth; can you really take all that in?

This greater truth seeks to find its way to all of us, much more than we try to find it. No one has to remain in the dark, and we are not left to our own limited resources. Rather, Jesus has come to put us in touch with everything that there is in knowing God, his Father.

After all, in following Jesus, we are following one who had equal status with God but didn't think so much of himself that he had to cling to the advantages of that status. What do we cling to in order to defend our own identity and status?

The freedom found in discovering who we are to God makes

even our greatest affirmations and highest achievements pale into insignificance. He knew us even before we knew him. His agenda is sourced in love. It is a love which perennially overturns everything in our lives so that he can get the worst in us to become the best of us.

The reality of knowing

I loved learning that *credo*, the Latin word from which we get 'creed,' actually comes from the Latin word for heart, *corda*. So when we say the Apostles' Creed, 'I believe in God the Father Almighty, and in Jesus Christ his only Son our Lord,' we are saying that we know this not merely with our heads but also with our hearts.

To say, 'I believe' is not to say 'I know,' in the same way that I know this is Tuesday. Rather, just as David the psalm maker did, we must honestly admit to God that, 'What you are after is truth from the inside out...' Here is truth that we know much more deeply than our minds can reason out.

It is that truth of the heart that the poet Wendell Berry calls 'knowing by cherishing, knowing by affection, knowing by heart.' The best part of life is like that. After all, you cannot understand love with your mind alone. You cannot reduce your love for another person to a formula. I would be very hard pressed to prove the dearest, most precious, most cherished parts of my life by mere reason alone.

At the same time however, I am willing to bet my life on them. We know love because of the dynamic synergy that occurs between the head and the heart of remembering and cherishing.

Next year I will turn sixty two. Over the past few years, I have become increasingly aware of something that has brought both disquiet and discovery. In all my years of formal theological training, my understanding of God has largely been shaped by what I am trained to think, rather than being taught how to think.

After I graduated from college and began working in a church, when it came to the sermons, I would either listen with an attentive ear or simply turn off and not hear at all. My training in what to think caused me to merely tick off a box about whether the speaker had impressed or depressed me. Anything outside my theological frame of reference would be met with ridicule and arrogance.

These days, however, things have changed rather dramatically. I have become conscious that God is not at all interested in my opinion about so and so; 'God pays no attention to what others say (or what I think) about myself or others. He makes up his own mind.'

There is a vast distance between what you have been trained to think and learning how to think, as there is a vast difference between what the head understands and what the heart cherishes. Learning how to think is like an explorer moving off the beaten path and turning a corner to a whole new world. There she encounters new vistas and contours, and hears sounds and voices for the very first time. It is scary and yet full of surprise.

It is like the excitement that had gripped her in her earliest years, but now, her entire world has been saturated with wonder and awe. What she had encountered in text books and lecture rooms is not lost, but now it all comes alive to her senses in a profoundly new way. And even though she followed traditions which placed her on the well-worn paths, she has also become unmistakably aware that going off the beaten track can lead to greater discoveries, both personally and professionally.

Similarly, it is like the farmer toiling away with scientific data on the relationship between the water tables and the land. The input of experts helps him produce more feed for his cattle and promote the health of the soil and grasses. Nonetheless, he has a titanic struggle with his intuitive desire to explore other paths.

These paths of learning fall well outside the scientific realm and push him deeper into the wisdom of traditional land owners. It is a knowledge permeated with a rich depth of insight, which demands of him the courage to take new steps into a strange, unmapped new land.

It is no different in the spiritual realm. Unique to each pilgrim, pastoralist or explorer is an innate restlessness to courageously struggle against the grain towards freedom. Life, especially the religious life, cannot be contained in an either/or approach.

Freedom is tasted when we begin to yield to a both/and rhythm, because the primary issue is not that our way is the right way or that our group has the monopoly on truth. Rather, learning how to think means not constantly filtering everything about God through the grid of the particular tradition in which we have been trained. True freedom often lies outside and beyond the box in which we have placed God. It is when we welcome at the table those who do not espouse the same well-worn doctrines as we do, or even sing the same songs.

Freedom is in knowing that when we walk away from that table, we have loved generously, listened honestly and served humbly, rather than depersonalising everyone if they did not agree with everything that we said. I have discovered that God is at home with me when I am not hoarding the spotlight by articulating what matters to me and my group.

It is simply coming to God naked, vulnerable, and transparent, with nothing else but wide open eyes and alert ears – being ready to listen and love. It is praying, 'Take what I offer, breathe on it; baptise it with your grace and give me light to see and the courage to disperse what impedes my ability to venture further in this realm of truly knowing. Teach me how to love those who represent differentness, even when I have assumed that because they are not from my group then they must not know you.'

Information technicians

In this reality of knowing we actually find that we are not very different to the religious leaders and scholars of Jesus' day. We may have well-grounded assertions and assumptions about God, but they can only be understood within a particular frame of reference and interpretation. Furthermore, much of our learning relates more to our capacity to memorize and download the appropriate information. If anything, we simply become skilled as information technicians. This will not enable us to grasp the potency of the knowledge of God.

If we constantly feel the need to defend God and provide explanations about him, it can be nothing more than a ploy to avoid meaningful dialogue and intimacy with God and with others, especially those outside our specific faith tradition. It is like presenting an opera in all its detail yet without music. All the content is there, yet without the vital ingredient. Similarly, music emerges from the very interior of our souls, and it's only when we discover the mutual compatibility between the heart and the head that communion between the two is richly restored.

The art of not getting lost on the way home definitely relates to finding ourselves off the beaten track. This is not adolescent behaviour, or throwing our life or our faith away irresponsibly. Rather, staying true to God means allowing God to take you and do with you whatever he wants.

Any truth we hold that does not set us free into the life which God intended, cannot be truth sourced in Jesus who is the truth. This truth will lead us out of our smallness of thinking and into the most surprising scenarios with God.

This is precisely why we must ask if the Gethsemane prayer was only so that Jesus could secure us a reservation in our new home? Surely not! The art of not getting lost translates into 'not what I am wanting but what you want God!' Even though our faith journey may be unsure and unsteady, we actually do begin to grow. We become more and more aware that God has been attempting to get us to listen and see things differently.

This means that he also wants to empty our hearts and heads of lots of religious clutter with no bearing on living a transformed life. This way we can begin to look and behave a lot more like Jesus. Being at home with God is finally living for the first time, just like Jesus lived, because reality is viewed from God's much larger and bigger perspective, not from our own narrow outlook.

Learned ignorance

Five centuries ago, Nicholas of Cusa made a big contribution to theology with an idea he called Learned Ignorance. He wrote, 'God is the unknown infinite who dwells in light inaccessible' and so God's greatest gift to us is 'to know that we do not know.' In Nicholas' scheme, the most foolish people are those who think they know. Their certainty about what is true not only pits them against each other, it also prevents them from learning anything new. And that is truly dangerous knowledge.

They do not know that they do not know and their unlearned ignorance keeps them in the dark about most of the things that matter. To know that you do not know is the beginning of wisdom.[2]

For there is more to knowing than knowing will ever know.

Without a shadow of doubt, the well-worn paths of pilgrimage and exploration demand our respect. However, if our theological and biblical education does not inspire an insatiable appetite to pursue God in places beyond our traditions, then we are merely treading the same tired old routes.

Some people say that they love music, but the very thought of attending a symphony is furthest from their minds. Their appreciation of the rich diversity of musical instruments is found wanting. To become aware of what is available in an orchestra will mean being exposed to the new and the unfamiliar, the surprising and the scary, the greater mystery and the marvel of music. This exposure will mean that they will never be the same again and their appreciation of music will not be so limited.

In the spiritual realm, to remain confined to what we have been trained to think will not only be detrimental to our capacity for personal growth, but will also impede our receptivity to the greater mystery of God. This does not mean abrogating everything we know, but about enlarging and enriching our capacity for more of God. God must not remain as an object of study.

God continually calls us out and further on in this new-found land of reality. Yet be warned, an opinionated head combined with an obdurate heart means that we will not be teachable in our quest to know him. God's pursuit of us is far greater and more intense than we could ever understand.

Painstakingly, God pursues us to grow up in him. He is intent on taking us beyond the confines of anything that fences him in. He houses us in his presence so that we become his habitation for all things whole and holy.

It was a revelation to me when I encountered a devout student of the Hebrew Scriptures in the New Testament who sought out Jesus for some resolve to his dilemma. Although religious through and through and a worshiper of Yahweh, he was unable to get his head around what he heard about this rabbi without credentials from Nazareth.

The conversation between him and Jesus does not tell us whether the enquirer was seeking an answer to a specific theological or religious problem. What we do know, however, is that this encounter bears all the fingerprints of God, the enigmatic teacher.

'If you do not know where you are, look at where your feet are,' says an old Buddhist proverb. He is with Jesus and this will keep us on our toes right to the very end. Jesus has come to light his fire within us. It is a fire which not only illuminates but also purifies all that would deny God being at home in us and us with him now.

This chapter invites us to follow the journey of a formidable Jewish theologian who had encountered this fire in the rabbi from Nazareth. He could see it in Jesus. He knew it was there straightaway, because he began to experience it in himself. And he knew that he had to be with this man.

It is a fire which burns but does not consume.

It is a fire which illumines but does not impede.

It is intriguing and inviting.

It is impossible to contain by any theological or philosophical rationale.

He knew that he must meet with this Jesus. His questions could only begin to unravel in the presence of Christ. This seeker was a well-educated theologian and respected member of the Sanhedrin. Somehow he knew that he could only see partially, yet he was hungry for more.

Carrying the weighty reputation as the 'teacher of Israel,' he had clearly accumulated and acquired significant status in the theological community of his day. However, in his faith journey something went awry. His religious education left him stranded with lots of scholarly notes, copious amounts of researched papers, but gnawing away inside his head and heart was 'O God, what are you trying to tell me?'

We too must be willing to go where this man headed, in order to find the truth of what it means to be in a relationship with God. I cannot underscore enough that God works best from the inside out, overhauling and undermining our well-thought-out ideas of who he is and what he ought to be for us. We may have begun well and have become steeped in our denominational outlook, but it does not necessarily mean that we are still staying true in our pursuit of knowing God personally and intimately.

If anything, routine often replaces running after Jesus, and predictability predisposes passion to be nothing more than hearing our own voice. We want to be heard and to be known, because we believe we have something to say. Yet God is still in charge of the universe and keeps everything ticking along even without our contribution. God is pleased when we are able to,

Love rather than hate

Dignify rather than despise

Serve rather than take

Listen rather than speak

Worship him rather than ourselves.

Nothing ever originated with us. God is ever-patient in bringing order out of the chaos of our life.

Get up. Let's go. It's time to leave here

If we don't appreciate that the New Testament was not initially written in chapters and verses, with headings and sub headings, we can so easily miss what has preceded a story. This is especially true of the gospel narratives when it comes to the explosive energy associated with the arrival of Jesus. The first century Mediterranean world was confronted with:

Jesus went to Galilee preaching the Message of God: 'Time's up! God's kingdom is here. Change your life and believe the Message'. (Mark 1:14-15)

Mark confronts readers with a never-ending fire hose of challenges spilling out throughout his narrative. He decisively declares that his story is about how God would become king. And it is Jesus who is definitively giving expression to God's authoritative reign to all the would-be-power brokers oppressing and exploiting people made in the image of God.

The message is that entrance in the new age to come is both accessible and available in Jesus. It begins now; therefore change your life and enter a learning curve which you can never fully work out. Don't bother attempting to box God into a narrow category or group which purports to have the correct answers, while people are being turned away from the God revealed in Jesus. No one will find their true place of being, until they are home with God. If anything, they will simply find themselves home alone...

This radical rabbi from Galilee sowed all sorts of new ideas about the kingdom of God. While crowds followed Jesus, other players in the kingdom drama, the religious experts, tried to put Jesus in his place. They exercised their authority to make sure that this itinerant teacher was not peddling anything heretical. They had credibility and position, having been trained in what to think regarding Judaism. Their entire worldview was the Temple and Torah; they were the thought police!

In the first century, religion, politics, economic and social life were one huge melting pot, with no clear separation. And because the people of God were under foreign overlords, the mood was that of revolution.[3]

Pre-empting Jesus' arrival, a band of Jewish revolutionaries fought under the banner of 'No King but God.' Therefore, anyone amassing a following would be seen as a prime candidate for an all-out investigation. It was in this hothouse of terrorist activities and religious subversives that Jesus made the startling announcement, 'Time's up! God's kingdom is here. Change your life and believe the Message.'

In effect: 'Get up. Let's go. It's time to leave here.' The reality is that those who had ears to hear began to follow Jesus, which sets the stage for one such principal investigator. His name is Nicodemus. And yet there is something almost awkward, if not clumsy, about his inquiry.

There was a man of the Pharisees sect, Nicodemus, a prominent leader among the Jews. Late one night he visited Jesus and said,

'Rabbi, we all know you are a teacher straight from God. No one could do all the God-pointing, God-revealing acts you do, if God wasn't in it.' (John 3:1-2)

I like Nicodemus because he was a heavyweight when it came to God and Judaism, with the onerous title: the teacher of Israel. Yet despite his reputation, stirrings of faith were awakened by this un-credentialed rabbi. Discussions with fellow rabbis concerning this Nazarene, for some reason, had not adequately answered his concerns. For Nicodemus, nothing could be tucked away and put to bed. His nights were becoming much longer than his days.

There beats within the heart of this man what I can only describe as a divine 'must.' Each of us know of that moment when the intuitive or gut feeling demands that we have to do something. There is something going down at a deeper level, a knowing that cannot be put to rest until something or someone is found. Indeed, every step is an arrival. For Nicodemus, it was an urgency of such magnitude that neither research nor study could assuage his troubled soul.

Perhaps Nicodemus was merely checking up on Jesus' theology, simply putting Jesus in his place like the rest of the religious experts of his day would do. However, this man who was seeking light approached Jesus under the cover of darkness. He was moving to the beat of a different drummer, and perhaps like Bono would have said: 'And I still haven't found what I'm looking for...'

A disturbing diagnosis

In the gospel stories, enquirers asked Jesus his view on topics, like a kind of entrance exam. However there is a conspicuous absence of Jesus doing this with his audience. Could it be that God didn't come to start a brand new religion, but rather, to reinforce his original intentions about this thing that we are not very good at: namely relationship. There is no doubt that God and only God can honestly say, 'I know you and have known you from the beginning.'

And is it not also patently obvious that God has always intended that when we own his image and likeness, then we are truly at home with him, reflecting his nature?

Many of us spend a lifetime trying so hard to earn status, self-belief and identity. As Nicodemus met Jesus for the first time, even the darkness of the night could not conceal his unmistakable quest to be known and heard. Perhaps this theologian had come to the conviction that he didn't really know God, like this rabbi Jesus did! Could he have recognized that a god who is perfectly understandable and conforms to the human intellect has been domesticated and is not the living God at all?

Inwardly, Nicodemus had already taken a stand; now outwardly he was taking steps to see where that would leave him. But Jesus did not answer the specific content of Nicodemus' determined preamble. Of course, Jesus knew where he wanted to lead Nicodemus, because he specializes in helping people see in the spiritual darkness, far greater than the night that envelops them both.

When God makes sense of the darkness for us, we can learn to truly see. Jesus pushed his inquirer to go much further than what he even knew he was capable of grasping hold of. The hour was at hand: the darkness of the theologian's intellect was met by the brilliance of the light of Jesus' heart and mind.

Jesus responded:

'You're absolutely right. Take it from me. Unless a person is born from above, it's not possible to see what I'm pointing to – to God's kingdom.' 'How can anyone,' said Nicodemus, 'be born who has already been born and grown up? Re-enter your mother's womb and be born again. What are you saying with this born-from above talk?' (John 3:3-4)

In the serve and volley of this communication, Jesus' cryptic comments were challenged by Nicodemus' literalness, as he attempted to salvage some sense of dignity and intellectual pride. This was definitely not shadow boxing. The blows were hitting their intended mark. Nicodemus required all the theological muscle and fitness that he could muster for this serious bout in the ring with Jesus.

Would Nicodemus come away a different person? Would the blows which have struck him make a lasting impression? In one corner was Nicodemus the graduate theologian, man of letters, 'teacher of Israel'; in the other corner, was the vulnerable, transparent and responsible God-man Jesus.

Dropped into Jesus' conversation was something mentioned for the very first time in the New Testament. This was clearly a signal to pay attention, a preview of so much more to come. It was the reference to being 'born again,' 'born from above.'

Jesus' answer was so enigmatic that it highlights the limits of language to describe and define the most profound human experience. He was making a disturbing diagnosis of humanity's true condition. And if Nicodemus could grasp what Jesus was on about, it would be thoroughly enlightening. In the context of Israel's worldview as the chosen people of God, this expression 'born again' was disturbingly provocative and more sharply focused than we may imagine.

The Judaism that Nicodemus and Jesus both knew had a great deal to do with being a child of Abraham. Racial identity was a primary identity marker for any Jew. Provocative as ever, Jesus was saying that God was bringing into being a new family in which ordinary birth would not be enough. The same word here can mean 'a second time' and perhaps most significantly, 'from above.' John had already hinted in his opening chapter that the initiative is exclusively God's.

...he made to be their true selves, their child-of-God selves.

Children, who were born not of natural descent, nor a human decision, or a husband's will, but born of God. (John 1:12b-13)

The expression 'born again' in church tradition, is always associated with being saved from sin. However, in the lively discussion which Jesus has with the learned theologian, the concept of sin is conspicuously absent. We do not have the full record of the conversation that ensued between Jesus and Nicodemus. But even our well-worn doctrines cannot project back into it predictable answers. Therefore, let us reflect...

Could Jesus have been pointing to the idea of 'new creation'?

The expression 'new creation' is normally associated with the apostle Paul and like the expression 'born again' it only occurs twice in the entire New Testament (2 Corinthians 5:17 and Galatians 6:15). In his letters to the Christians at Corinth, Paul wrote of 'new creation' in the context of reconciliation and Jesus becoming sin for us. Although Paul does not specifically use the term 'born again,' inherent in his understanding of the new creation is that the initiative lies totally and entirely with God.

God had come and begun the work of bringing into being a new humanity, a new creation through Messiah Jesus. As for matters pertaining to racial heritage and belonging to the right family, for Nicodemus, as for all of us, it is all about 'grace' and not 'race.'

Nicodemus had to undergo a total and radical change

In his earnest efforts to be a good, religious person in order to acquire sufficient standing with God, Nicodemus was a devout student of the Hebrew Scriptures and Judaism. However, Jesus was insistent that Nicodemus needed a new set of eyes to see things, especially regarding God. Jesus said to Nicodemus: 'It's impossible to see...'

In effect, he was saying, 'You do not have a clue, nor do others.

It is more than merely removing your glasses or acquiring degrees, or switching text books. Nicodemus, your training has created this confusion. It has led you this far, but it cannot take you any further, especially when it involves seeing God.

'Yes, you do have a desire to truly see in order to know me. And yet your blindness cannot be corrected through education. Teachers have their place, but none can ever take the place of what you must experience with me. This is not a one-off mystical experience; learning how to see is an unending story. Transformation of sight is my specialty and it is a gift for those who are willing to be born from above.

'I want to bring every person to the place of asking me to be with them and them with me. Once you find your heart and head are at home with me, then your entire body will give expression to a life formed from within. Your life will begin looking like the image and character that I have always wanted for humanity, taking the shape of Jesus, the most authentic human being ever.'

What do you mean?

When Nicodemus resorted to a bald literalness in response to being 'born again', a rather comical scenario ensued of him imagining that he, an old man, had to return to his mother's womb. Jesus responds, 'When a baby is born, the one who does all the strenuous work is not the baby; it's the mother, the one giving birth. Nicodemus, this is also true of God at work to bring about new birth.'

In this one-on-one conversation, note that Jesus used the second person plural, 'you', when he said, *'You must be born again'* (John 3:3,7). He was implying that Nicodemus was representative of all humanity, Jew or Gentile.

It is as if Jesus was saying,

'Regardless of educational rank, religious accomplishments or family status, everyone, including you, Nicodemus, must be reduced to a helpless, defenseless and powerless infant, a baby. Your life must be utterly dependent on God and utterly identified with God. The fact of life is that birth is where we all begin.

'If a person is on the wrong track, it is no use running faster. You must begin at the very beginning. Nicodemus, you have some standing among your peers, but now it's time for you to discover how God wants you to stand for the rest of your life.'

You're not listening...

The scholar theologian continued to get much more than he bargained for with Jesus. Not only did Nicodemus discover that he was limited in his capacity to see, but also that he had impaired hearing. To grasp this reality of knowing, not only would he require new eyes to see but he would also require new ears to hear what Jesus was getting at. This is foundational to this new way of knowing and living.

You're not listening. Let me say it again. Unless a person submits to this original creation – the wind hovering over the 'water' creation, the invisible moving the visible, a baptism into new life – it is not possible to enter God's kingdom. So don't be surprised when I tell you that you have to be 'born from above' – out of this world, so to speak. You know well enough how the wind blows this way and that. You hear it rustling through the trees, but you have no idea where it comes from or where it's headed next. That's the way it is with everyone 'born from above' by the wind of God, the Spirit of God. (John 3:5, 7-8)

The night wind was whistling and perhaps even rattling the windows of the place where Jesus and Nicodemus were meeting in. The wind (after all, the same word in Greek for 'spirit') blows where it will. You can hear the wind, you can feel it all around you, but you cannot see it. You don't know where it comes from or where it is going. So the mystery of God's activity, God's Spirit, is not predictable or controllable. What Nicodemus was searching for was God, transcendent and mysterious. God not confined to human reason, religious rules or even the best theology. The reality is totally other.

Breathtakingly, God revealed himself to humanity as helpless and utterly dependent in Jesus the baby born to Mary and Joseph, conceived by the Holy Spirit. In this defenseless state, Jesus lived his life in the will of his Father, co-operating daily with the Holy Spirit. He embodied what it means to allow God to be at home in a human being. So Nicodemus had to make up his mind:

He could go on explaining how God works according to his Pharisaic training or he could allow himself to be reduced to a state of unreserved helplessness and dependency, as God educated him in the reality of knowing. Becoming attuned to the nudges and nuances of the Spirit's speech, there was a noticeable impact on the mind and heart of Nicodemus. The holy wind of God had been stirring him up.

I haven't let go of you

Nicodemus' final questions to Jesus were 'What do you mean by this? How does this happen?' The discussion closed abruptly, but it was not the end of the story. Nicodemus' first steps toward Jesus were certainly not his last. In fact, the next time we meet Nicodemus in John's narrative, he had progressed a little further. Out of the long dark night, now into the light of the day, his stand was a little more public.

If you have viewed the Mel Gibson classic *The Passion of the Christ*, you may have seen Nicodemus at the trials of Jesus. He was present with the leaders who were ferociously fired up, inciting the crowds with venomous vitriolic to get rid of the Nazarene. So Nicodemus stood with his peers as the temple guards reported to the high priests and Pharisees about Jesus. Nicodemus had to face his own ambivalence: he could follow Jesus or remain stalled as a fearful sympathizer among his colleagues.

The [temple] police answered, 'Have you heard the way he talks? We've never heard anyone speak like this man.' The Pharisees said, 'Are you carried away like the rest of the rabble? You don't see any of the leaders believing in him, do you? Or any from the Pharisees? It's only this crowd, ignorant of God's Law that is taken in by him – and dammed.' Nicodemus, the man who had come to Jesus earlier and was both a ruler and a Pharisee, spoke up. 'Does our Law decide about a man's guilt without first listening to him and finding out what he is doing?' But they cut him off. 'Are you also campaigning for the Galilean? Examine the evidence. See if any prophet comes from Galilee.' Then they all went home. (John 7:46-53)

Had the rhetoric of Jesus simply touched the temple guards with an idle sense of curiosity? But this is not just chance or mere coincidence; this is surely a God-incidence. God is sovereign and he knows where we need to be, and he will use whatever means to get our attention. It's as if these Temple guards had taken a crash course in apologetics! Their testimonies definitely ring true as witnesses pointing to Jesus.

Nicodemus' worldview is enmeshed in Torah and temple, the two key symbols in Judaism, so the implications of following this rabbi from Galilee were unimaginable. Yet he knew that he could not have a foot in two boats, nor could he walk on water, yet. He wanted the respect of his colleagues but that wouldn't answer his unresolved questions about God.

It all started with that conversation with Jesus on the night that he could never forget. Jesus had not let go of Nicodemus, and Nicodemus was now alone and perplexed, crying, 'O God, what are you trying to tell me?'

The reality of being 'born from above' was throwing open to him a much larger world which demanded abrogating all his understanding of Israel's God and the Messianic age. It could have a heavy impact on his own senior status as the 'teacher of Israel.' Nicodemus' world was unraveling right before his eyes. His scholarly acumen was of little worth in acquiring a true knowledge of God. Despite his education he was far from home and lost.

The scholars had long held the view that history was divided into two periods: 'the present age,' and 'the age to come' when God would at last act decisively to judge evil, rescue Israel, and create a new world of justice and peace. Now Nicodemus was faced with the arrival of one who said, *'Time's up! God's kingdom is here. Change your life and believe the Message'.* (Mark 1:15)

Nicodemus had to face swallowing his pride and pocketing his fears among those whom he has worked with, prayed with, worshipped with and held the same deeply entrenched views about God. What would he do? After that decisive moment of moving out of his comfort zone to rendezvous with Jesus on that night, he now needed to take even bolder steps into the broad daylight of faith in the Messiah Jesus. Nicodemus was still playing it safe, although he was speaking up.

His eyes were compelled to consider Jesus, even while his ears were singed by the words of the Temple guards and his own colleagues. In the cut and thrust of peer pressure, he had to decide between the Nazarene and his professional colleagues. His conscience pricked him with the very words which he spoke with Jesus...

'We all know that you are a teacher straight from God. No one could do all the God pointing, God revealing acts you do, if God weren't in it.'

Nicodemus must have been musing, 'Jesus, I really cannot get my head around you. You have not studied or graduated from our theological academy. You are not even a member of our group. My confidence is steeped in our heritage and all that Israel represents.

All this is what makes sense to me. Need I remind you, Jesus, of our credentials?'

They had everything going for them – family, covenants, revelation, worship, promises, to say nothing of being the race that has produced the Messiah, the Christ, who is God over everything, always. Oh, yes! (Romans 9:4-5)

'Yet you are asking me to be reduced to a helpless baby so I can become a member of the new creation. This is totally unthinkable! What do you mean by this? How does this happen?'

Nicodemus would have been keenly aware of the conversations and stories circulating, and the daily news releases about Jesus among the people, not just in the synagogues. Jesus would never have been far from the thinking of Nicodemus, who would not have been oblivious to the trials and horrendous beatings. He must have watched Jesus suffering and stumbling on the Via Dolorosa on his way to death.

I love you Jesus

I will say again, it is the humanness of Jesus that comprehensively deals with our human-mess. In order to grasp this, let us look at the closing drama of Nicodemus' story in the nineteenth chapter of John's gospel. This is exactly where I believe God wants us all to come to.

The art of not getting lost on the way home is about being at home with God right now, not just later. But in this crisis, who would want to be associated with Jesus anyway? Even his closest companions had abandoned him, hiding away for fear of the Jews. The disciples' muddle-headed and malformed faith incapacitated them and collectively they closed ranks against Jesus.

What could Jesus offer Nicodemus now? What counsel can Jesus bring to the searcher's deep question, 'O God, what are you trying to tell me?'

Yet this competent theologian who came to Jesus seeking light under cover of the darkness makes a courageous step in Jesus' final hours. Nicodemus has wrestled with darkness and it has brought things to the surface which this learned man may have kept concealed for a very long time. Paradoxically, in his encounter with Jesus' death, Nicodemus faces his own.

Death well and truly descended upon Jesus; he was now in the darkest of nights and in the depths of hell. Yet light was enlightening the heart and mind of Nicodemus. The true light which enlightens every person had come and was beckoning him to keep on moving toward Jesus. Indeed, revelation has broken through:

Joseph came and took the body. Nicodemus, who had first come to Jesus at night, came now in broad daylight carrying a mixture of myrrh and aloes about seventy five pounds. (John 19:39)

Did you catch those two words 'broad daylight'? All along Nicodemus has been moving with God to God. Stuttering steps admittedly, but step by step, he has been yielding to the prodding and probing of the Holy Spirit. We must never give up on anyone, for God has a perfect timetable and strategy to reveal himself to anyone. The surreptitious nocturnal visitor was now out in broad daylight at the grave of Jesus.

Now Nicodemus knew that his own life was peripheral to the bigger story unfolding. He came loaded down with personal issues and concerns at his first meeting with Jesus, but now he is loaded up with more myrrh and aloes than required. Such a large amount of spices would be certainly more fitting to anoint a king for burial. Initially, he could not see, now grace has opened his eyes to see the revelation of Israel's king in the man from Galilee.

Faith is not synonymous with certainty. If anything, it is about daily making a decision to keeping our eyes and ears wide open to the clues which God lays on the path of faith. We must make our way with him even when it means encountering death's dark shadow. If we cling to tradition, it may only burden us instead of releasing us into the arms of God, who is far bigger than any faith tradition.

This final scene of Nicodemus' life speaks volumes about his love for Jesus. Seeing as he does, Nicodemus loves Jesus for who he is, not for what he can get out of him. It's not about healing, words of prophecy, words of wisdom or teaching, or confirmation as to whether he has been selected to be a part of this kingdom movement. Jesus is dead. But…Nicodemus loves Jesus for Jesus.

Nicodemus is saying: 'I love you, Jesus.' When a person gets to that place in their life they will stand forever, unshaken and unassailable to anything or anyone. They will be immersed in the reality of knowing that:

Nothing living or dead; angelic or demonic; today or tomorrow; high or low; thinkable or unthinkable – absolutely nothing can ever get between us and God's love because of the way that Jesus our Master has embraced us. (Romans 8:38-39)

For Nicodemus to come out in broad daylight demonstrates that he has a new capacity to see and a bold humility to be seen. Like Nicodemus, we must learn how to see. An admission of our blindness is not easy; indeed, it takes a divine encounter. In John's words in the opening page of his gospel, we need to be: *'children… not born of natural descent, nor human decision, nor of a husband's will, but born of God'* (John 1:13). Then it is that we will find ourselves taking new steps in following Jesus.

Watching someone moving towards their death, watching them dying, powerfully reflects Nicodemus' own journey of enlightenment. This is the coming home that I am speaking about: home with God now!

Whatever list of questions Nicodemus may have carried ultimately died in the death of Jesus. The daily choices we make are not normally viewed in the framework of 'life' and 'death.' Most of our decisions do not seem that important, and yet life and death are before us every day. We must learn to see that death is often the slow process of giving ourselves to what does not matter.[4]

True dying is appropriating the death of Jesus on our behalf. Then it is that we begin to live. God challenges us all to love God for God and not for selfish reasons. That is the kind of person he wants to show off to the world. We must simply love God for God's sake – not for what we can get out of him or what he can do for us...

Tidy and neat is really not how we meet, okay!

God is not encompassed and circumscribed by human words. He is bigger and more real than anyone's description or creed or religion or theology or church. Nicodemus became aware that the mind does not come alive until it meets what it cannot comprehend. Following Jesus and embracing this new way of knowing demands a healthy imagination. We need both roots and wings, both memory and metaphor. To see as Jesus did we can't be stuck in the old order, controlled by old boundaries and a limited line of sight.

It is curious that Mark's closing words in his original story of the resurrection are, 'And they were afraid' (Mark 16:8). This is not a polished conclusion in finishing his narrative, nor does it present the disciples in a favorable light. And yet, this is precisely how Mark wanted to end his gospel. He wants to leave us feeling the fear and doubt because like Nicodemus and the disciples, we too have to find faith by walking our own journey. It is not having all the boxes ticked. Everything does not have to be tidy and neat.

The life of Nicodemus, like all people on this journey of faith, is not self-directed or self-governed. Rather, this God knows and calls each of us by name, even while we may imagine we are unknown to him.[5]

The unrelenting God

Nicodemus' dilemma is paralleled in the New Testament by that of another scholar of all things Jewish, namely Saul of Tarsus. Saul was a Pharisee of Pharisees, way ahead of his contemporaries when it came to God thought and God talk. However, his letter to the Christians at Philippi shows us that when God is at work in a person's life, he is unrelenting.

The very credentials these people are waving around as something special, I'm tearing up and throwing out with the trash – along with everything else I used to take credit for. And why? Because of Christ. Yes, all things I once thought were so important are gone from my life. Compared to the high privilege of knowing Christ Jesus as my Master, first hand, everything I once thought that I had going for me is insignificant – dog dung. (Philippians 3:7-8)

That same person whom Nicodemus had met up with, the carpenter's son, had now assaulted Saul's entire world. Despite being theologically advanced he was awash with ignorance about God's designs for him. Saul, who became Paul, had studied, served, worshiped and taught God. However, now his eyes were opened to Jesus.

To be reduced to a sense of utter helplessness, we must be willing to let go of stuff that makes us look successful and good. If our posture is one of 'Look what I have to offer you, God,' or 'Look what I can do for your Kingdom,' then we have not come out of our box at all. Worst of all, we are trying to put God in that same box. God is not a commodity in whom we invest for the sake of our own grandiose plans. Because God is unrelenting love, he will painstakingly clear our blurred vision, and we will see it yet. But like Nicodemus, we must love God for God – nothing else, nothing more and nothing less.

And like Paul, we must give up all that inferior stuff, which accords us with status. We give it up so that we can know Jesus personally, experience his resurrection power, be a partner in his suffering and go all the way with him to death itself (Philippians 3:10-11).

To follow Jesus and to allow his teaching to come alive in our being, we must know that God does not abandon humanity. Even when the world appears to suggest his absence, God remains committed as God. Behind all the apparent evidence, God loves us, wants us, desires a full and joyful life for us, and loves us with an everlasting love. We experience this when we allow God to be at home with us.

Many people regret how they were never encouraged in the area of education, leaving them with a galling sense of inferiority and stupidity. Yet God himself is willing to educate them in the curriculum of his enigmatic ways. Once in a personal relationship with God, they become insatiable, devouring text after text of genuine substance, which years before they would have been oblivious to. This is a profound evidence of being a new creation, 'born from above.'

Conclusion

Nicodemus opened the windows of his world to the fresh wind of the Spirit of God. Yet letting the breeze in can be very inconvenient, especially when we have just gotten our life tidied up, labelled and sorted into neat piles. However, the wind blows where it wills. God cannot be domesticated or tamed; he remains decisively God, for us and with us, all the way to the end. We can sometimes feel that we are all over the place with God and that is when we need to listen to him say, 'It is okay.' We need to rest in his okay, okay?

The great British journalist, Malcolm Muggeridge, after a life of scepticism, became a believer when he saw God's unconditional love for the world in Mother Teresa's love for the homeless and dying on the streets of Calcutta. The impact of love transforming ugliness into a beauty beyond compare caused Muggeridge to write many years later:

It sounds crazy, as it did to Nicodemus who asked how it was possible to be born again. Yet it happens: it has happened innumerable times. Suddenly caught up in the wonder of God's love flooding the universe, made aware of the stupendous creativity that animates all life—every colour brighter, every shape more shapely, every meaning clearer, every note more musical, above all, every human face, all human companionship, recognizably a family affair—all irradiated with the same new glory in the eyes of the newly born.[6]

Nicodemus was surely newly born. His burning question, 'O God, what are you trying to tell me?' had found its answer in the incomprehensible Jesus of Nazareth. Jesus is none other than God and the true Adam for all humanity. He is the giver of heaven's breath in the Holy Spirit, which fills our hearts when God is at home.

Like Nicodemus, we no longer allow anything or anyone to cast a shadow on the monumental discovery that the long walk is worth it all, especially when God is our companion. A companion whose demand is that we let him love us and change us from the inside out.

That change is more than a nice touch-up spiritually. It is a radical renovation of heart and mind, as his identity is formed in us. This identity is wrapped up in allowing God to make his home in us.

Our fourth chapter is shaped by the question, 'O God, is this really you?' If we have somehow lost our way, it may be because we have confined ourselves to mastering the thousand and one chess moves to be played out so that God really does not have his way with us.

Endnotes

1. George Hunsinger's comments on Church Dogmatics in *How to Read Karl Barth: The Shape of his Theology* (Oxford: Oxford University Press, 1993), 27-28
2. Barbara Brown Taylor, *Learned Ignorance* (The Christian Century, 1 June 2001)

3. NT Wright, *The New Testament and The People of God* (London: SPCK, 2002 (6th impression)).

4. Brett Younger in *Feasting on the Word: Preaching the Revised Common Lectionary, Year A, Volume 1* –'Advent Through Transfiguration', David L Bartlett and Barbara Brown Taylor, ed. (Louisville, Westminster John Knox Press, 2010) 341.

5. Walter Brueggemann, (*The New Interpreter's Bible, vol. 1, The Book of Exodus*, Nashville: Abingdon Press, 1994p. 719)

6. Malcolm Muggeridge, *Christ and the Media* (Cambridge: W. B. Eerdmans Publishing Company, 1977), pp.74, 75

Chapter Four
'O God, Is This Really You?'

There was a young girl in an art class, drawing away, as did everyone in the class. The teacher moved around the room, and then stopped next to the young girl and asked, 'What are you drawing?' The young girl responded, 'God.' The teacher said, 'Well, no one knows what God looks like,' And the girl replied, 'They will in a few minutes.' (Sir Ken Robinson)1

The normal thing would be a picture of a house with colourful flowers in the garden and the bright sun up in the sky. But this young girl has other things going on in her fertile mind: 'Let's take on God!' Unembarrassed, she simply says it as she sees it. Children are so unafraid of telling it like it is. Conversely as adults, we are much more prone to defend ourselves, always wanting to be right in everything and avoiding looking awkward or ignorant at all costs.

From the very beginning the plan was that all sons of Adam and daughters of Eve would reveal pictures of God through the canvas of their own lives. It was no afterthought or plan B that we should reflect God's image in the world. But to accurately portray that likeness, every human being is invited into an immensely personal relationship with God which demands that we stay in love with Jesus all the way.

Jesus has to factor in the equation, because there is and will never be anyone else who could properly represent God. This is why Jesus really matters if we are to maintain our focus for the long journey of faith. Augustine said it well: 'The moment we say we understand God, this is nothing more than an admission that we have yet to meet the true and living God.'

Therefore whatever our grasp of all things pertaining to God, the data must always lead us to the person of Jesus. When we look at him, we see the God who cannot be seen. The simplicity of the young girl's response to her teacher evokes the question: 'What image do we carry in our hearts and heads of God?'

The picture that we carry has significant bearing on the art of not getting lost on the way home. This God, revealed to us in Jesus, accommodates our limitations, so much so, that he is not put off by our question, 'O God, is this really you?'

A perennial procedure

In my pastoral role, I have had the luxury of involvement with many people, which has led to surprising conversations. These encounters have shaped me in learning how to see God. Too many times to recall, folk have surreptitiously cornered me at a gathering and confronted me with a volley of questions, normally prefaced with: 'Have you got five minutes? I have some God questions to throw your way. You're the one who has studied and has the degrees, therefore...'

Without question, there has always been the expectation of a return serve. Yet the majority of these people were not brand-new followers of Jesus; instead they have been long standing members of churches. They are often people who have given huge investments of time, money and commitment to church life.

Over the years they have been wounded by being unable to speak openly about their issues about God. Or when they did speak, immediately they had been assailed with stock-standard scriptural references which they could not repel because of fear of being told, 'It is heresy to question God and his word.' And so they had patched their wounds, with grimacing efforts to maintain faith and be good Christians who do not rock the boat.

Their unanswered questions filled the cabinets of their minds and hearts. Everything was tucked away, yet spilling out occasionally, with the hope that the discerning person might stop and attend to them. It seemed that they were always expectant, regardless of the right or wrong answer.

Keen to see myself as a walking concordance and the cure of ailing souls, I armed myself with sufficient theological artillery and bible bullets to match. I would stand ready for the ensuing encounter with the returning serve. I was affirmed by the fact that people felt comfortable with me in their struggles, but retrospectively I see that the affirmation merely stroked my ego. Unbeknown to me, God was setting me up. He knew my penchant for waxing eloquent ad nauseam as a fountain of knowledge.

My homeland is Australia and it is not uncommon to be awakened to the morning sound of warbling magpies. One of our most accomplished songbirds, the Australian magpie has an array of complex vocalisations. The parallel is that we pastors and leaders, theologians and lecturers, are often enamoured by the sound of our own warbling, it is a kind of a mag-piety! Take it from me that where delusion abounds, confusion much more abounds.

The good news however is that dear friends reminded me recently, 'Van, you have changed so much.' As I received this with open arms and a grateful embrace, they added: 'You were always so full of yourself.' These are definitely true friends! They have stayed the journey with me for many years.

Much to my chagrin they pointed out that they had told me this many times, much earlier in our relationship. Quite clearly, the truth of Jesus' words, 'the one having an ear to hear; let him hear,' had found no resonance with me. Listen I did, but more often to my own warbling! However, change has come and for that I am truly thankful.

Among the many contributing factors to this change has been the discipline of writing my first book, The Art of Not Disappearing. Bit by bit, blow by blow, God has always wanted me to face the stark reality of my own inner world, because otherwise I was actually missing glimpses of God in the people that he brings into my world. Yes, I would meet with them, and yet, not really see them.

The reason was that what I was looking for in the faces of those whom I met, was purely a reflection of my own image. I wanted to be congratulated for coming up with the right answer. Regretfully however, I was forfeiting the opportunity to see and hear people for who they are, not just for what I could do for them, and in that way failing to see the God picture.

As I stayed rigidly Pharisaic, the questions asked simply pressed buttons in me for specific categories with prescribed scripts and responses. I had a predisposed stance on how God must fit into my 'god-shaped' box.

The box was supported by cleverly constructed scaffolding with systematic texts to fortify the idol of my ingenuity. But God was not fazed, even though he knew all about this. For he had the perfect timing for the box to fall apart and for me to undergo his thoroughgoing procedure: a Pharisectomy! This procedure is never a one-off event; it is a continuum over a lifetime with God.

What I am talking about here perfectly describes how we can so easily get lost along the way. Yes I was into God but it was only about the things that mattered for me. All of us who take it upon ourselves to be 'god' in other people's lives get lost along the way with God and others when we...

Control in order to prop up our own insecurities

Counsel so that we can subtly work out our own issues

Manipulate so that we can maintain the art of disappearing, remaining unknown

Perform in order to present an idealised image for others and God.

Supernatural surgery which originates with God always has two components: perfect timing and revelation to follow. The revelation was simply two words...

Intellectual idolatry

These two words, 'intellectual idolatry,' spoiled my Pharisaic posture. I sulked for days. And because of my unwillingness to respond to God, not only was I miserable, but for three days my dear wife and family had to bear the brunt of my childish bouts. 'Intellectual idolatry,' I objected defensively to God, 'How could this be?' The one who came with unfailing love and mercy to reveal my hidden agenda was immediately set upon by my self-justification.

Admitting to intellectual idolatry was easier to manage while it remained only in my head and I kept it entirely to myself, with the luxury of thinking that everything was being processed and worked through. Of course this was none other than self-delusion. However, God's strategy for surgery caught me out.

It was not to be over and done with in a moment of praying and confessing. It had to do with people. Stick around people long enough and not only will you catch glimpses of God, but also of the very best and the very worst of what we are capable of being.

As I listened to people's personal struggles, I would find myself wiping the tears from my own eyes. Often they would say, 'You are such a sensitive person with a tender heart,' but if only they knew!

Tenderness and sensitivity were aspects of my character, but they were not well formed; they were often driven by wrong motives. Yet God knew me thoroughly and he placed people in my life to unravel my world so that he could perform supernatural surgery.

As I truly began to look into their faces, I was being taught how to see. Equally, I was learning how to listen as I heard beyond their words to their hearts speaking. The self that I had defended, to prove to everyone that it was good and great, found no voice, not even a whimper.

This steep learning curve of actually listening, threw me headfirst into a recurring refrain in both the Christian mystical and the Buddhist traditions. It had to do with 'staying awake,' or in three words, 'being fully present'. This was something which I was so unschooled in.

I was quite prepared to be an information technician, dispensing text after text, outperforming others in order to secure centre stage. It was not a conducive environment for 'staying awake' or 'being fully present.' I was so conditioned to wanting life to be only about me as I envied and lusted after prominence. Tearfully, I stammered out, 'I am blind, but now, I am starting to see.'

Through conversations with people, grace invaded my life. This was God's surgery to remove my arrogant intellectualism. As I lingered in this place with God, I became the inarticulate one. Under God's hand the reality broke through that when procrastination gathers momentum, revelation will be blocked. And when revelation is blocked, transformation cannot flourish. I gave in to the battlefield of my mind, to the theatre of my thought world.

Knowledge postured itself like a sentinel guarding against surrender to Jesus

Yet my obstinacy began to melt in the welcoming embrace of the Master

Deeply entrenched defences could not hold out under the powerful force of love

For he is love

His love is the only power which can change the human heart and mind

My fragility was the new knowledge and the way of wisdom.

Although my acute sense of lostness threatened to consume me whole, it was punctured by in-breaking light. Light began to lead me to the one who had found me in the first place. He was never distant; he was always near. After all, he is the ever-present, fully present God for us and with us, all the way to the end of our days. Jesus alone can show me God's image to carry as long as I have breath and being. When grace is at work, eyes begin to see.

And I did see my real need of listening, learning and forging a greater openness in the furnace of vulnerability with others. Much more than ever before, I know I must keep returning to the place of a child:

I'm telling you, once and for all, that unless you return to square one and start over like children, you're not even going to get a look at the kingdom, let alone get in... (Matthew 18:3)

Have you ever wondered what took place in that classroom, when the pictures were collected by the teacher and put on display for all to see? Would the young girl's painting of God be worth a thousand words?

That answer must be left to the world of pure imagination, something which God employs often in bringing about transformation in human hearts and heads. This is especially so in the steep learning curve of learning how to see him. Every person who was brought by God into my world broke down my conception of him and others.

God really does not want us to get lost along the way as we seek to follow him. Lost to ourselves, lost in our posturing and parading in order to be noticed and applauded for our contribution to the Kingdom of self! Enter the flying nun...

The flying nun

After completing a four-day intensive training seminar called 'Evangelism Explosion,' I was headed south to do some teaching in a church in Melbourne, Australia.[2] As I sat down in the plane mulling over the lessons prepared and the talks to be given, another person also found her seat. Her clothing spoke volumes, more than a red carpet Oscar nominee or Stella McCartney label.

The passenger who accompanied me for this two-hour flight was comfortably dressed in a brown habit and a veil covering her head. She would have been in her seventies. Inwardly I was turning over the recent scenarios painted by the presenter at the evangelism clinic about approaching the lost and locating them on a scale of seekers and non-seekers. I was raring to implement the strategies which I had memorised. Here was a prime candidate, I could win her soul to Jesus.

When she had settled in, I didn't need to ask her what she did for a living, because it was patently obvious! However I began to think about the stories that I could share with colleagues upon my return. Forgive me, and remember that we are usually a victim of the last seminar or conference that we have attended...I was utterly convinced that this was a God-appointment. This was indeed true, but not as I expected.

I assumed that she was oblivious to the person seated next to her, a fully armed witness of the gospel. Undoubtedly, she needed to hear the gospel, and who better to communicate this message to her, but me? But before I could get my spiel working, she turned to me and asked, 'What do you do with your life?' Without delay I set sail for the broad expansive seas of the gospel presentation, bringing her in my wake. She listened and listened and listened, making no response, no gesture at all.

Transfixed, she was totally present to me. Even when I went over propositions, one-liner formulas and strategies, she did not miss a beat. Proof texts began to pile up as I extracted them from the extensive filing cabinets in my mind. She was captivated. Her face was open and there was no look of incredulity or offence. I was certainly in on a winning scenario.

However, before I could get to any sort of closure in order to secure her confession of the sinner's prayer, she simply stared at me, and her look spoke a thousand words. At that moment it dawned on me that when I had occasionally glanced at her face, her eyes were soft and alive with light. Her artistic hands with slender fingers touched my arm. After what seemed like an eternity of silence, she asked me for my name and then she said:

'Van, what an immense privilege you have had, to be able to study the Scriptures. And you have been given the opportunity to learn how to listen to God speaking to you, so that you could feel his heart towards those who do not know his love.' From that moment on, I was smitten; I was gone. Internally, I was tripping over my thoughts and stumbling over my feelings.

God was the object of my vocation, the one to be studied. What sort of language was this 'learning to listen to God'? 'Feeling his heart towards others…?' Studying God, formulating essays about him, wrestling with concepts within creedal statements, delineating the finer points of ancient and modern theologians and languages I knew. But learning to listen to God, for God and not for anything else?

As I was eager to escape, a reprieve came: the flight attendant with our meals. I got stuck into mine, but glanced out of the corner of my eye and noticed that my travelling companion had declined hers. 'You are not eating?' I said to her. She generously smiled, 'Would you like my meal?' I assured her that I had enough, though I was not entirely honest. Of course I could have eaten her meal; the lamb was tender and the cheesecake was tasty. She said, 'Van, I am fasting.'

Immediately, the name Harry Houdini, the great escapologist of the twentieth century came to mind as I sought cover. A sudden rush to the men's room meant running away from her.

And where was I going to run to anyway?

I was only running away from myself.

And really, how far does that get you?

I knew my attempts at running were futile. They would simply lead me back to where it all began, headlong into God – who, by the way, I had realised was fully present dressed in a brown habit and wearing a veil. What a picture of God!

She was fasting and I was grazing.

She was generous towards me and I was stingy with her.

She was honest with me and I was not honest with her.

I wanted a statistic for my gallery of converts.

She saw me as someone who was privileged to have sat at the feet of the Master.

After devouring my meal, there was absolutely nowhere else to go. She had remained motionless and quietly attentive to me with all my fidgeting. She knew that I knew that I had to speak to her after having so readily served up a shrink-wrapped portion of the gospel.

It was not that she had not listened; she had.

It was not that she told me to mind my own business; she hadn't.

She waited.

So without knowing what to say, I blurted out, 'How did you get into your order?'

She said first things first: 'My name is Sister Mildred.' For the next fifteen minutes she left me spellbound, explaining how she had heard the voice of the good shepherd many years ago, as a young girl. It was the good shepherd, who gave her a heart to love the poor. She spoke of her involvement in community work so that she could make a difference for those unable to live a quality life in the inner city suburbs of Melbourne. Fasting was a regular routine in her life. She said that her burdens were too great and so many that she too must learn to listen to the good shepherd.

She longed to love the people with whom she was constantly involved, so that they could find their way home to his heart. I joined 'The Order of the Good Shepherd.' Her face was marked with lines of unmistakable joy even though she had walked many a long day and had spent even longer nights with the broken, the lonely and the lost. It was me in the classroom. Any questions which I may have had regarding God, especially, the 'O God, is this really you?' one, Sister Mildred's portrayal blew it out of the plane.

Over and over again my pictures of what God was supposed to look and sound like were being dismantled. Radical alterations were taking place, up so high in the clouds, 'where the things of earth grow so strangely dim.'

The process was disturbing, as she disarmed me well and truly. The absurdity of my arrogance unfolded right before my eyes. I had been so adamant that I was going to win her to Jesus! How could a nun, lost in papacy and the Vatican, know what I knew about Jesus?

We prayed, I cried. She laughed and I died (metaphorically). I kissed her face and she touched mine with her hand. She said she knew I was in God's hands!

I have often pointed out to students who enrol in theological or Bible college that they have come not to learn answers, but to discover the right questions. Slowly, I have begun to realise that God doesn't always want us to pull out a proof text to prove his existence. Notice how the serpent in the very beginning asked Eve, 'Did God say...?' He didn't waver about the reality of God.

My flying nun story well and truly showed me how much we can resign God to the background while we take centre stage. God is not behind the scenes while we play god. His best canvas is often not the well-structured, highly polished demonstrations that we can produce. Yes, there is a place for excellence, but we may need to accept that God exceeds our expectations of him, because he is more in the midst of the chaotic than in the neatly choreographed scripts which we make him perform in.

We are so much into managing life that we forget how to live and enjoy it. This is especially evident when things are complicated and messy. I wonder as well, whether God views chaos and order the way we do anyway! God is speaking all the time, and is active all the time, even, or especially in the silences. It is when we learn to be comfortable with the silences that our awareness of God's presence and voice become more real to us.

Sister Mildred's silences on the plane spoke volumes to me. I was fresh out of the starting blocks with the starter's gun still ringing in my ears. I was pumped with zeal and armed to the back teeth with knowledge, but it was not the kind of knowledge which informed me that I am not god. Her silences were God's way of confronting my warped pastoral pathology, my own need to provide everything that relates to him in tidy prescriptive formulas. 'Take this and hear that.' The scaffolding of my god-construction wobbled and lurched under the sheer force of irresistible love on that evening flight.

I needed to be exorcised of all that had made me the major player and God the understudy, waiting in the wings for my direction and lead. My explanations had rendered the inner receptor of my spirit inactive, and my hearing was dull and inert. I was alert to my own voice, but not to the voice of the one who can roar and thunder when he speaks.

On that airplane God came in the still small whisper of Sister Mildred. After four days of a seminar, I had lots to communicate. But when Sister Mildred did speak to me, her words found their mark: 'Your heart is good but your motive was unwise. Do not be afraid to be yourself with God and others.'

It was the last time that I would ever see Millie. In writing this book, her story hit me between the eyes. The Spirit of God reminded me, 'When you first began with Jesus, he had made up his mind to be at home with you. Millie was right on the money; be yourself and be at home with him.'

'Do not be afraid'

Each of us I am sure has had those moments of hearing uncomfortable truth. I was exposed and unable to find suitable apparel to cover my pathetic frame, yet I also realised that it would be more embarrassing to try to cover up. So don't leave your hat on, whatever that hat represents; go the 'full Monty' with God. Otherwise, you are simply admitting to being really afraid and ego-centred deep down. This is usually when the chaos of not been in control kicks in.

My well-rehearsed speech, right down to the very best illustration, merely amplified how I was fired up with unholy zeal. My formulaic approach to the person sitting in the chair next to me was ridiculous. What I had originally thought would be the finish line, the conclusion to the conversation, left me tongue tied. I was rendered defenceless to the probing and wounding of God.

Paradoxically this descent into chaos was very much of God. His work was to bring about my undoing, even if it felt like darkness and despair. If we are to acquire a heart of wisdom, it is in learning to explore and glean from both the light and the darkness.

I am God, the only God there is.
I form light and create darkness,
I make harmonies and create discords
I, God, do all these things. (Isaiah 45:7)
God is there, to brood and bring to birth eyes that see and ears

that hear the words, 'I AM is with you.' In essence, wisdom is about handling life on God's terms. Sister Mildred's words, 'Do not be afraid' arrested my attention in a new way that was hard to grasp. It is such a familiar expression, occurring frequently in the scriptures.

Was the message, 'Get yourself ready; revelation is about to hit you. It's not about you; it is about what God wants to be to you and with you?'

A fresh assault was breaking into the small-mindedness of my egoistic ways. Our assumptions about understanding God's ways constantly need overhauling. In the Greek translation of the Hebrew Scriptures there is a fascinating aspect which adds further colour to this phrase, 'do not be afraid':

In that day it will be said to Jerusalem:
'Do not be afraid ['take courage[3]], *O Zion:*
Do not let your hands fall limp.
The Lord your God is in your midst,
A warrior who saves.' (Zephaniah 3:14-17a)

The prophet is clearly saying: 'God is in this, get ready for what he is going to do with you and for you.' The words will strengthen you so that God can perform his activity in you which will make you 'fearless ones.' God is preparing us to learn to live in awe and wonder on a daily basis, rather than with our small minded and irrational fears. 'Do not be afraid' is so much more than a psychological battle of fear versus faith, though that can be part of the equation.

When eyes and ears are attuned to God in readiness for him, not to get something from him or even to do something for him, we may find ourselves enveloped in intimacy with God that will enlarge, enrich and alter our entire perspective.

Therefore, 'Do not be afraid' catapults us into places where God wants to take us so that he can go on doing with us what he has always wanted to do through us. So don't be surprised if the next time you step out of your door you find God dressed up in a different guise!

A puzzling picture: for the first time

For a moment, imagine Jesus in the classroom. When the teacher of his day asks him, 'What are you drawing?' his answer is like the young girl's: 'God!' Like the young girl, Jesus would also give his audience a picture of God. There is no doubt that his response would have been met with incredulity, offense, cries of blasphemy and scandal. It would be most profound and yet intensely personal.

We can't deny that in the first century Mediterranean world, Jesus' picture of Messiah, God and God's ways, did not conform to anything his hearers would have understood as strictly orthodox. The multitudes were waiting for Messiah to emancipate them from foreign powers. They had been waiting for centuries for God to come with divine visitation in order to overthrow the oppressive power brokers. But...Nazareth of Galilee...really?

The crowds gathered and as they listened to Jesus, they became aware of a whole new spin on the tried and tested doctrines of their religion. They had to make room for a picture of God who can only inaugurate his kingly rule through utter vulnerability and apparent defeat. Think about it: who follows a man on a donkey, let alone on a cross? The religious experts were sure that this Jesus was on a collision course with the Judaic mind-set.

Even Jesus' forerunner, John did not make it any the easier:
Here he is. The Lamb of God who takes away the sin of the world. (John 1:29)

For the audience gathered to hear John the Baptist, this might have been a puzzling utterance. It is the first and only occurrence of these words in the Scriptures. They would evoke the image of Passover or sacrificial lambs offered on the altar, a familiar practice based on passages from the Torah requiring such a sacrifice for the putting away of certain kinds of sin. These could be called 'lambs of God.'

In the twenty-first century it's hard to appreciate how bewildering this phrase might have been for first century hearers. The benefit of hindsight and centuries of Christian scholarship allow us to readily interpret 'the Lamb of God' as Jesus' sacrifice on the cross. This picture is crucial evidence for the doctrine of atonement: Jesus 'the Lamb of God who takes away the sin of the world.' John the Baptist's audience, however did not have the advantage of this Christian lens. They were hearing this cryptic language for the first time.

Out in the wilderness, the crowds were keen to check out whether the Messiah had come. For John, this messianic personage was in the crowd. The one for whom they were to look was symbolised as an animal! Yet an animal representing people, kingdoms and nations is not at all uncommon in ancient literature and for that matter, right up to the present day: as in the symbol of the eagle for ancient Rome, the lion for the United Kingdom, and the bear for Russia.

Similarly, political cartoonists depict political parties through the symbolism of animals: the elephant for the Republicans and the donkey for the Democrats in the United States. However, in the context of the Jews suffering under the oppressive regime of Rome, John's puzzling word picture would have evoked consternation and confusion. A defenceless lamb is not a hero-like image, and could even offend a Jewish audience.

The idea that a human being could ever be sacrificed in an expiatory manner, treated that is, as an animal, was repugnant in Jewish culture where animal sacrifice was quite explicitly a substitute for human sacrifice. Therefore, John's symbolic language of the coming Messianic figure as 'the Lamb of God,' would not necessarily generate expectations of deliverance and salvation.

Surely John would have been far better off depicting the Lion of Judah. This somehow has a better ring to it. The lion is rapacious and terrifying – far better in terms of confronting Rome's might and power. Then again, prophets are meant to be provocative.

His words were not spoken into a vacuum. Within the grand Hebrew narrative the bigger story of Exodus and the wilderness story had a double aspect. On the one hand was judgment and God's displeasure, but on the other hand, it ushered hope and healing. For God had brought spectacular deliverance from foreign oppression out in the desert.

But... 'Look. The Lamb of God who takes away the sin of the world'? Would this engender hope to look to the coming one in their midst as the prophet had spoken, or would it simply result in wish-filled dreams being vanquished on the arid waste of the wilderness floor? Would this Jesus figure just be another unsuccessful revolutionary? Or can we pursue further lines of inquiry about 'the Lamb of God'?

As we keep in mind the art of not getting lost along the way home, another answer is forthcoming. It is seen on the canvas of the painter/prophet Isaiah.

An insightful interlude

In the ancient world many Jews were Messiah watchers, eagerly waiting, hoping against hope that Messiah would come and bring down the oppressive foreign overlords. In her exilic 'home' Babylon, Israel was called to get ready, for God was on the move, coming to act on her behalf. In the starkest and darkest of times Isaiah paints word pictures which portrayed God bringing about Israel's liberation.

He was beaten, he was tortured,
But he didn't say a word
Like a lamb taken to be slaughtered
And like a sheep being sheared
He took it all in silence.
Justice miscarried, and he was led off –

And did anyone really know what was happening? (Isaiah 53:7-8)

The picture painted by the prophet appears to bear no resemblance to a heroic deliverer. Nevertheless, did you notice that the word 'lamb' is mentioned? And the context is rich with a cluster of themes: vicarious suffering and redemptive purposes, as well as images of injustice and irony. Admittedly, for centuries scholars have argued much about the identity of the figure depicted by the prophet.

Is Israel the 'suffering servant?'

Is it perhaps God himself?

Or is it some personage who can only be fully understood centuries later through the medium and message of John the Baptizer?

None of these interpretations can be readily dismissed. As much as opinions vary and outcomes are diverse, other factors must be considered. This quandary is highlighted by the prophet himself when he asks of Israel:

Who has believed our message?

And to whom has the arm of the Lord been revealed? (Isaiah 53:1)

By all accounts, Isaiah's message fell on the deaf ears of incredulous listeners. Even the revelation of God's mighty power to emancipate the Jews from exile as he had done many times before in their history was revealed to ears that did not hear, and eyes that saw but were not seeing. Hebrew scholar, David Clines suggests that throughout Isaiah chapters 52:13 to Isaiah 53:

...silence is maintained, speech is avoided, by kings (v. 15), by witnesses (v. 8) and by the servant himself (cf. v. 9); the poem is about seeing, not hearing, so it is about vision rather than verbal communication.[4]

Isaiah does not specifically use the expression, 'the Lamb of God.' Nevertheless, Isaiah's pictorial language affords us with a graphic depiction of one whose sacrifice will not be in vain. Jews believed that in the offering of lambs, sins were atoned for.

So we have gleaned some insight, but it is only an interlude before something even more astonishing. It is astonishing, because God thought of everything that would keep us from getting lost when our human ingenuity is insufficient.

The Jewish scroll of Isaiah continues to speak, but we find ourselves apprehended by a non-Jew centuries later. It is a man in search of the sacred, that is being at home with God. His story unfolds for us in Luke's second volume, The Acts of the Apostles in the New Testament:

Nothing is ever wasted

'...at noon today I want you to walk over to that desolate road that goes from Jerusalem down to Gaza.' He got up and went. He met an Ethiopian eunuch coming down the road. The eunuch had been on a pilgrimage to Jerusalem and was returning to Ethiopia, where he was minister in charge of all the finances of Candace, Queen of the Ethiopians. He was riding in a chariot and reading the prophet Isaiah.

The Spirit told Philip, 'Climb into the chariot.'

Running up alongside, Philip heard the eunuch reading Isaiah and asked, 'Do you understand what you're reading?'

He answered, 'How can I without some help?' and invited Philip into the chariot with him. The passage he was reading was this:

As a sheep led to the slaughter,

And quiet as a lamb being sheared,

He was silent, saying nothing

He was mocked and put down, never got a fair trial.

But who now can count his kin since he's been taken from the earth?

The eunuch said, 'Tell me, who the prophet is talking about?'

Philip grabbed his chance. Using the passage as his text, he preached

Jesus to him. (Acts 8:25-35)

Two figures were out in the desert on the road that runs from Jerusalem to Gaza. One was an evangelist with the early Christian communities called Philip, schooled in listening to the voice of God. By asking God, 'teach me to hear you,' he picked up the frequency of God's speech and now found himself in the company of a non-Jewish African. The Ethiopian eunuch was in his chariot, immersed in the Jewish scroll of Isaiah 53.

This eunuch was drawn to the Jewish God, although his life had been enveloped by Roman decadence and the immoral mystery religions of the first-century Mediterranean world. He had travelled to Jerusalem to hear and to see more about the God of the Jews. However, he was clearly an outsider and would never be embraced by fellow Jews. Judaic instruction was insistent that he could not become a proselyte; there would be no place for him in Judaism.

And yet the man was absorbed in reading Isaiah. He did not have a clue what the ancient prophet was saying, but God knew that he needed a teacher. Philip also didn't have a clue what his next stop was going to be or what he would be doing next. If we do not want to lose our way with God, we must learn to embrace the gift of uncertainty. We will save ourselves a lot of unnecessary pain and anguish if we do this earlier than later. Uncertainty is much more about the ways of God than we realise!

The eunuch's search had left him with many unanswered questions, so he asked Philip, 'Tell me, who the prophet is talking about?' 'Was the prophet Isaiah writing about himself or someone else?'

Philip launched into an explanation of how Israel's story from Abraham through the prophets was reaching its climax in a servant who had come to accomplish God's will. Luke, the author, was clear that, 'Phillip preached Jesus' to the eunuch. Here is God searching for those not at home with him. The servant whom Phillip is speaking about would have stupendous implications for the Ethiopian.

For Philip and the early Christian community, the one whom Isaiah has portrayed is none other than Messiah Jesus. He is John the Baptiser's 'Lamb of God.' Just as Isaiah's picture led the eunuch to investigate the Jewish scroll, so he and Philip find themselves in the larger story of God and his purposes for all humanity.

Getting more than you bargained for...

Always with God there is much more going on. Tom Wright captures it so well:

The one through whom the long night of Israel's exile would arrive at its new dawn, [and] with it the promise of blessing for the world, of a new covenant (Isaiah 54) and a new creation (Isaiah 55) – and, with that, a blessing even for outsiders and foreigners, and yes, even eunuchs (Isaiah 56) is now available.[5]

Isaiah heralds the good news...

Make sure no outsider who now follows God

Ever has occasion to say, 'God put me in second class, I don't really belong.'

And make sure no physically mutilated person [eunuch in Hebrew] is ever made to think, 'I'm damaged goods. I don't really belong.'

For God says:

'To the mutilated [eunuchs] who keep my Sabbaths

And choose what delights me and keep a firm grip on my covenant,

I'll provide an honoured place in my family and within my city

Even more honoured than that of sons and daughters.

I'll confer permanent honours on them that will never be revoked'.
(Isaiah 56:3-5)

The Ethiopian eunuch's pilgrimage had reached its climax, and yet quite clearly it had only just begun. Irony and insight is all over his story. His answers were not found in Jerusalem; God's timing and place for revealing his face to this man were out on a desolate stretch of desert road.

Just like the many pilgrims over the centuries who had heard God's voice like fresh water to a thirsty soul in the searing temperatures of the desert, Isaiah's words would have been drunk deeply by this new member of the family of God:

And as for the outsiders who now follow me,
Working for me, loving my name,
And wanting to be my servants –
I'll bring them to my holy mountain
And give them joy in the house of prayer.
They'll be welcome to worship the same as the 'insiders',
To bring burnt offerings and sacrifices to my altar.
Oh yes, my house of worship
Will be known as a house of prayer for all people. (Isaiah 56:6-7)

God had orchestrated the perfect place, the perfect timing and the right person to make himself known to this seeker. The unnamed Ethiopian came home to God, and then continued on his faith journey. For a season he was lost, but now he found a home with God. Whatever faith he had in the past had now been illumined so that he saw that the God who had been drawing him could be known through the Messiah Jesus.

It is clear that the 'Lamb of God' image associated with Jesus in the gospel of John takes us to the very heart of the prophetic portrait of Isaiah 53. This picture from Isaiah's canvas was transformative for the Ethiopian eunuch, answering his dilemma, 'O God, is this really you?' But there is still one more occurrence in the world of the New Testament concerning this 'Lamb of God' imagery.

Mirror, mirror on the wall, who has the power after all?

Often when we encounter the pictures in the book of Revelation we tend to forget why they are there. Many complain recklessly,

'Revelations – all those visions, they are so bizarre.' However, in this bold piece of apocalyptic literature, we discover that the writer's habitual orientation and vocation are summed up in the words, 'I, John, the one seeing and hearing' (Revelation 22:8). In other words, John lived in a state of readiness to hear what God wanted to say to him for the churches under his watchful oversight.

One of the many complicated issues facing us in the book of Revelation is our tendency to isolate the visions from the auditions which occur alongside each other in the flow of the language.

In other words, what John was seeing tended to be consistently followed up with what he was hearing. The expression, 'I saw and I heard' throughout the apocalypse is recurrent.

John had to wait for God to make clear what he was saying to him through the pictures he was given. Therefore, what John 'hears' and what he 'sees' all relate to God's purposes for the churches. This is true not only for the first-century Mediterranean world, but also for us now.

After the prophetic messages to the seven Christian communities, the curtain is lifted up for the prophet and the recipients of the messages to see and to hear what God reveals. Immediately John asserts 'A door is opened into heaven...', here is the revelation unfolding...

I saw a scroll in the right hand of the One seated on the throne. It was written on both sides, fastened with seven seals. I also saw a powerful angel calling out in a voice like thunder, 'Is there anyone who can open the scroll, who can break its seals?' (Revelation 5:1)

The very nature of any apocalyptic document is essentially about unveiling or revealing. 'A door is opened into heaven...' and John encountered someone sitting on the throne with a scroll in his hands.

The significance of the scroll must not be underestimated, because it represents God's purposes and plans for this world and the next. It relates to the unfolding of the history of humanity; finality, judgment and destruction; the bringing into being of the new heavens and the new earth; and ultimately, all that constitutes 'new creation' fulfilment.

Even if this is all that you grasp from this apocalyptic document, it can change your life forever. Because the picture of one on the throne proclaims clearly that God is still very much in control of everything. In the world of John and fellow believers, two pictures sharply emerge and collide. One is the threatening image of first-century Rome, broadcasting an entirely different message, especially about who was in control. Remember, Caesar is Lord!

However, the other picture which John was privileged to see and communicate to his churches shows God as Sovereign and Lord over all. The significance of such a picture aligns powerfully with the words of Jesus: *'As in heaven, so on earth…' 'As above, so below…'* (Matthew 6:10).

For the beleaguered Christian communities living under the shadow of powerful Rome, life was a choice between either praying and seeking to live out the gospel, or saving their own skin and that of their family. In the first-century world the very mention that 'Jesus is Lord' would be tantamount to treason. Yet for those who loved Jesus, unquestionably, God was actually still in charge!

The glorious picture of the throne would provide courage and engender hope to hold on to their faith and love for Jesus. But there is still more to be grasped about the picture which John saw.

There was no one – no one in Heaven, no one on earth, no one from the underworld – able to break the scroll and read it.

I wept and wept and wept that no one was found able to open the scroll, able to read it. One of the elders said, 'Don't weep. Look – the Lion from Tribe Judah, the Root of David's Tree has conquered. He can open the scroll, can rip through the seven seals.'

So I looked and there surrounded by throne animals, and elders, was a Lamb slaughtered but standing tall... (Revelation 5:3-6a)

Deeply contrite and broken hearted, John heard a voice which exhorted him to look and listen beyond his tears. This is something which prophets know all about: weeping, seeing and hearing, then weeping again! It is almost a vocational rhythm. What the distraught prophet heard was the good news that the Lion has overcome and is able to open the scroll and its seven seals.

This paradox pushed John to the end of himself, drawing our attention to not only a deliberate change in the image from lion to a lamb, but also with the Greek word for 'lamb.' In John's gospel, John the Baptizer speaks of *'the lamb of God taking away the sin of the world'* (John 1:29). The word which John uses there is of an 'an adult sheep.'

Conversely, in Revelation, John of Patmos employs a word conveying the picture of a little lamb.[6] This picture is designed to overthrow all our ideas of might and power. Locate yourself for a moment in the ancient world, with Rome as the power-broking bully and the oppressor of people. John' message is singularly subversive and utterly radical, because Rome has been overcome by Mary's little lamb! This lamb's mission is not only to remove sin from the human race, but also to restore justice and power through his weakness and humility.

Hence our question: 'O God, is this really you?' 'How does this make any sense?'

There is power in powerlessness

Vulnerability and transparency, weakness and humility, are not normally on the agenda at the tables of world leaders. The way authority and power are wielded so that good may triumph over evil is problematic to say the least. After centuries of so-called progress, propelled by the ideology that only might is right, the world can scarcely see 'might and right' is the way God intended.

However when world leaders are enlightened to see humanity made in the image of the true and living God, they will be empowered to seize God's kingdom mandate about what constitutes true authority and power. This image has been authenticated by none other than Jesus Christ. It is he who will continue to defy power in its present expression of world dominance, just as in the first century world.

I am thoroughly persuaded that the most formidable power ever to change a human life is Jesus, and his expression of power is none other than love. When exercised appropriately, it neither exploits, corrupts, nor dehumanises the status of men, women and children. In the overall scheme of things, love makes sin unnecessary and takes it away.

Centuries after John's day, this picture of Jesus as the vulnerable God would grip the minds and hearts of two hymn makers of the church. Charles Wesley exuberantly proclaimed:
'Veiled in flesh the Godhead see, hail the incarnate deity!' Hundreds of years after Wesley, enthralled by the same depiction, Graham Kendrick wrote:

From heaven you came helpless babe,
Entered our world, your glory veiled
Not to be served but to serve
And give your life that we might live.
This is our God, the Servant King,
Who calls us now to follow him
To bring our lives as a daily offering
of worship to, the Servant King.[7]

In contrast to power-hungry Rome, the unveiling of the picture of Jesus as the Lamb of God was intended to both startle and surprise us into learning how to be at home with God.

Startling and surprising

It startles because Jesus comes for every person whose life is manacled to sin-enslaving patterns and stunted, self-absorbed ideologies. In other words, this person is lost, but not to God.

It surprises because when Jesus is allowed to transform a life from the inside out, then who we are and what we are living for, emerges. It is the image of God unveiled in vulnerable, transparent and responsible human beings in love with God and his purposes for this world and the next.

It is startling and surprising because Jesus the lamb will not conform to any of the world rulers. He is not like any other conqueror. Long ago, Isaiah declared to the oppressive power brokers of Babylon and to his fellow countrymen, 'Nothing and no one can compare with him.'

It is startling and surprising because the conquering Lamb won through death. It was not by capitulation to Rome's edicts, nor by militant might and violence. Rather, the Lamb prevailed because he knew that in the hands of his Father there is a scroll which must be opened. Its opening demands a perfect life lived and a dying which would summarily cancel death's reign over every son of Adam and daughter of Eve, both now and forever.

His humanness for our human-mess

Therefore if humanity and history are ever going to change, the scroll cannot remain sealed. This slain Lamb is the only one who is able to reveal the plan of God for the entire flow of human history. In his living and dying, we may each learn to mirror true power. Mary's little lamb epitomises true power in meekness and majesty.

To be startled and surprised reminds us that awe and wonder are integral in the art of not getting lost on the way to Jesus, our home. Jesus is the living revelation of all that represents true God and true humanity.

Your life is a journey you must travel with a deep consciousness of God. It cost God plenty to get you out of that dead-end, empty-headed life you grew up in. He paid with Christ's sacred blood, you know. He died like an unblemished sacrificial lamb. And this was no afterthought, even though it has only lately – at the end of the ages – become public knowledge. God always knew he was going to do this for you. (1 Peter 1:19-20)

Christianity dares to believe that God materialized in human form in one ordinary Jew, bearing the name Jesus. Beyond these contradictory elements which defy rigorous philosophical, scientific and theological enquiry is the issue of how we can love a real person. God becoming a human being is not something we clinically measure, critique or analyse. Rather it has to do with the person that we meet. And Jesus is that person.

He is the quintessential, perfect expression of God and personhood.

He is the authentic human being.

Until we humble ourselves and surrender to this portrait of God in Jesus, faith cannot truly be born, nor can our humanness deal with its human-mess. When we take the first nascent steps towards Jesus, stirrings will occur at all levels: intellectually, emotionally, spiritually and physically, as to how we will live and die, learn and laugh, hate and love.

These are all purely symptomatic of the birthing of our true humanness made alive in Jesus. Therefore the question, 'O God, is this really you?' is answered by the power of transforming love in Jesus:

The transformation began the moment Jesus left his Father's side to come to earth.

The transformation was actualised when he became a human being.

Our transformation occurred when Jesus allowed God to put our wrongs on himself who never did anything wrong, so that we could be made right because of him.

John discovered that this is precisely the place where true power is revealed. We need to focus on the picture of the Lamb of God in selfless surrender to the will of him whose vision of a new creation turns everything right side up.

Through Sister Millie, God set me up. I wasn't particularly interested in her, only in giving her my portrayal of me, and I had assumed that I already knew the answer to the question, 'O God, is this really you?' anyway.

The Ethiopian eunuch must have been carrying the burden of finding God all his life. To his question, 'O God, is this really you?' Philip did not hesitate to speak of Jesus.

Jesus – the faces of people in my world

Jesus – Sister Mildred – God the flying nun

Jesus – John the Baptiser's 'Lamb of God'

Jesus – Isaiah's suffering servant God

Jesus – Phillip and the Ethiopian eunuch

Jesus – Mary's 'little lamb' –vulnerable, transparent and taking responsibility for every human being.

Conclusion

The question, 'O God, is this really you?' will be a constant throughout our very human journey. At the end of the day and the long night, you may still want to know what God looks like. This is where faith comes into its own. Our questions may never be exhausted, but faith functions like a receiver in readiness for the revelation which God wants to impart creatively and freely.

The reception of his revelation demands nothing less than absolute honesty. When honesty is the air we breathe, we cannot get lost. As God becomes more at home with us and us more at home with him, we find that we are becoming the person that he always intended for us to be.

God has no intention of absconding, even when we drop the ball or fail him or become too enamoured by our own achievements. God remains God and is utterly secure as God. He will always be in charge. Even though we know this is true, nevertheless, each of us can at times stumble along the way. Perhaps it is because we tend to suffer with the fearful final question, 'O God, will I really make it?'

Endnotes

1. Sir Ken Robinson, a talk on Creativity in Education, TED, 2009.
2. This clinic took place in mid 1989.
3. 'Tharsei - take courage. It occurs only seven times in the New Testament (Matthew 9:2, 22; 14:27; Mark 6:50; 10:49; John 16:33; Acts 23:11), and six of the seven are from the lips of Jesus. The exception is here' Walter W. Wessel, 'Mark,' Expositor's Bible Commentary, Vol. 8, (Grand Rapids: Zondervan, 1984), 722.
4. D. J. A. Clines, I, He, We, and They, (JSOTSup 3; Sheffield: JSOT, 1976), 43-44.
5. N. T. Wright, *Acts for Everyone Part 1* (Louisville: Westminster, John Knox Press, 2008), 135.
6. John 1:29 is ἀμνός and in the book of Revelation 5:6 is ἀρνίον.
7. Graham Kendrick, 'The Servant King,' ThankYou Music 1983, administered Worldwide by EMI.

Chapter Five
'O God, Will I Really Make It?'

John clinched his witness with this:
'I watched the Spirit, like a dove flying down out of the sky,
making himself at home in him.' (John 1:32)

'O God, will I really make it?' is a question that has been posed so many times and from so many people from different walks of life and differing ages. Some are students studying the Scriptures, while others simply need the assurance that they have not lost their way with God. Percolating away in our hearts and heads, we find faith and fear wrestling with this 'O God, will I really make it?' question.

We most certainly want certainty about crossing the finish line. Yet I have often wondered what Jesus would say to his disciples, as he embarked on his farewell journey to be with his Father once again. Would heaven as home weigh heavily in the conversations with his close friends?

We'd like to know that everything is neatly signed, sealed and delivered, our reservation is intact, and we will be safe. In order to make sense of this final question, I want to set the stage for our continuing faith journey together with the final words of the gospel accounts.

Matthew

Go out and train everyone you meet, far and near, in this way of life, marking them by baptism in the threefold name: Father, Son, and Holy Spirit. Then instruct them in the practice of all I have commanded you. I'll be with you as you do this, day after day after day, right up to the end of the age. (Matthew 28:19-20)

Mark

They got out as fast as they could, beside themselves, their heads swimming. Stunned, they said nothing to anyone. (Mark 16:8) [1]

Luke

What comes next is very important: I am sending what my Father promised to you, so stay here in the city until he arrives, until you're equipped with power from on high. (Luke 24:39)

John

There are so many other things Jesus did. If they were all written down, each of them, one by one, I can't imagine a world big enough to hold such a library of books. (John 21:25)

Imagine yourself in their position, with Jesus no longer physically present. In light of each account ask yourself, what would their focus be for the days ahead? Would it not be 'Get going and get on with living, cooperating with the Holy Spirit who is in you and with you'? 'Struggles and being stretched are inevitable.' 'I will stick with you right to the very end' 'It is okay not to have worked out everything about Jesus because there are not even enough books to provide all the information about him anyway.'

If you are still not convinced, Luke's second book captures Jesus' final words...

These were his last words. As they watched, he was taken up and disappeared in a cloud. They stood there, staring into the empty sky. Suddenly two men appeared – in white robes! They said, 'You Galileans! – why do you just stand here looking up at an empty sky? This very Jesus who was taken up from among you to heaven will come as certainly – and mysteriously – as he left.' (Acts 1:9-11)

Their attention is captured by angels and an empty sky. Jesus is taken away from them and yet he will return. Unquestionably the focus revolves around that man Jesus, and the issue of arriving or getting into heaven hardly factors into the equation. Therefore the question, 'O God, will I really make it?' appears to be out of place in the overall scheme of things.

Overwhelmingly, the message is of being empowered for witness work and radical obedience. It is being Jesus in the world. And for this to come to fruition, his followers must be unhindered in receiving the gift of the Holy Spirit. The Holy Spirit is promised by Jesus and imparted by his Father to every person who is in Christ, a gift which far surpasses any other gift we could ever imagine.

Yes, we can wax eloquent about getting saved, having our sins forgiven and being on our way to heaven. Yes, we can announce the wonder of spending eternity forever with God. Yet none of these truths will ever make any sense without the empowering, invasive presence of God the Holy Spirit being at home in us. For it is his intent to make us more like Jesus right now, as well as to break open Jesus' teaching about God, who we are and what are we living for.

Therefore our 'O God, will I really make it?' question pales into insignificance in the full light of knowing and allowing ourselves to be fully alert and actively cooperating with the Holy Spirit, right now and to the end of our days.

Meanwhile, the joyful anticipation deepens

Being at home with the Holy Spirit involves wholeheartedly accepting Jesus' life in us. His work in us is sourced in the power of love. As Eugene Peterson aptly comments:

For God put his love on the line for us by offering his Son in sacrificial death while we were of no use whatever to him. And we are never left feeling short-changed. Quite the contrary – we can't round up enough containers to hold everything God generously pours into our lives through the Holy Spirit. (Romans 5:8, 5)

The language of this life of love with God takes its cues no longer from a sightless and self-obsessed world. The new life that is ours in Jesus, seeks to keep us in step with the Spirit. When this life-shaping Spirit reality begins to become more like second nature to us, then the word obedience is no longer hedged about by 'shoulds' and 'oughts.' Rather, it is the desire to live life in love and loved by God.

This is why I have specifically chosen the opening quote from John's gospel:

John clinched his witness with this:

'I watched the Spirit, like a dove flying down out of the sky, making himself at home in him. (John 1:32)

This is exactly what Jesus embodied in his humanity. Jesus, the most authentic human being who ever graced this earth, walked constantly with the Holy Spirit and was always in the face of his Father, Abba.

Do you realise that because God loves humanity so much – to the extent that he became a human being – he wants to continue the same pattern that he had with Jesus, with every human being? Namely, living in us and being at home with us, right now!

In the full blaze of this reality, the question, 'O God, will I really make it?' exists because we have allowed ourselves to exchange the truth for a lie. We are deceived into not accepting just how loved we really are, and just how much God really wants to be at home in human lives. This is why we so desperately need the empowering presence of the Holy Spirit in our lives.

If we always carried within us the words spoken to Jesus by his Father at his baptism, 'You are my Son, chosen and marked by my love, pride of my life,' I believe we could go all the distance in keeping step with Jesus. That way the 'O God, will I really make it?' question would not stand a chance. Because we would know from our very beginning in Jesus that it could never be about earning God's love. Rather, it is welcoming the truth that God does not love us if we change – God loves us so that we can change.

For this very reason, our living can be characterised by the joyful, deepening anticipation of heaven breaking into our lives right here and now. This heaven and earth interaction will bring us the answer to the question, 'O God, will I really make it?'

That's why I don't think there's any comparison between the present hard times and the coming good times. The created world itself can hardly wait for what's coming next. Everything in creation is being more or less held back. God reins it in until both creation and all the creatures are ready and can be released at the same moment into the glorious times ahead. Meanwhile, the joyful anticipation deepens. (Romans 8:18-21)

Dual citizenship

All that pertains to my identity, my significance and vocational identity, what I am living for and where I am headed in my life, all finds its meaning in Jesus. From a human perspective, we need the appropriate identity documents. Over recent decades, stolen identities have caused great heartache for many people.

Proper documentation is no more obvious than when it comes to international travel. A valid and up-to-date passport is a must, and often to secure employment we need work visas. Many people these days carry dual or multiple-citizenship status to legitimise access to work and residence in many parts of our global village. This scenario is true on the natural level, but there is a spiritual parallel.

In Christ, we now also have the privileged responsibility of a dual status citizenship, on earth and in heaven. This does not mean that we become otherworldly and less human. If anything, we become more authentically human – just like Jesus – capable of intercepting heaven's communiques and resources. In this way our earthly perspectives on how to live, love, worship, serve and even die, undergo a massive re-evaluation.

The document which caught the attention of the church for centuries, often for all the wrong reasons, has unfolding scenes of worship in its pages. The songs sung in heaven were pivotal and imperative to the early Christian communities. They were never intended to eliminate the present, but to bring into sharper relief the truth about who is in charge of everything.

Heaven's songs are not primarily about Jesus' birth or life; the greatest cause for excitement is the death of Jesus, which *'has rescued every human being from going down dead end alleys and into dark dungeons. Jesus got us out of the pit we were in, got rid of the sins we were doomed to keep repeating.'* (Colossians 1:13-14)

When songs empower us, the joyful anticipation deepens. Hope is engendered in our worship, faith is energised in our daily living and love is infused in us towards the one who secured for all eternity our home in him in the new heavens and a new earth.

For this very reason Jesus dynamically sends us out into a world which God so loves, so that we may be:

A people not detached from others

A people alive to the reality of heaven's character

A people sent out as carriers of heaven's values, and

A people on a collision course with a world which refuses to allow God to be in charge.

Yes, we are on our way to heaven but that is not the end of the story. It is but the beginning. This is precisely why restlessness and rootlessness are part and parcel of the Christian spirit. As Augustine so significantly noticed, our hearts are restless until they find rest in God. That's the big point about God. It is God who is our true home, our 'eternal home', as the hymn puts it.

Therefore if we are to cultivate the art of not getting lost on the way home, we must stop, press the pause button and catch our breath. We need to listen to what the Spirit is saying to us as dual citizens, attempting to live out this combined heaven-earth reality now. There is nowhere else that we can go, nor anyone else who will help us make sense of it.

That is why it is time to embark, embrace, and be enveloped with the greatest gift that the Father and the Son have always wanted to give every human being, especially when it comes to making sense of home.

What do you mean?

Jesus and the Father always had in mind that the Spirit of God would literally invade us with his life, so that we could become increasingly whole and holy to the very end of our human story. That ending no one can adequately comprehend. In many ways, all that we had hoped and longed for will be surpassed by all that God is and has in his never ending story with us.

This interaction between heaven and earth is now to be the environment in which we live and breathe and have our being. How amazing it is that we have personal tuition by none other than the Holy Spirit. We are to be taught how to live out this heaven/earth reality now! And guess what? All our fees have been paid right up front by the lavish love of Christ.

That's why we have this Scripture text:

No one's ever seen or heard anything like this,
Never so much as imagined anything quite like it –
What God has arranged for those who love him. (1 Corinthians 2:9)

These words comprehensively spell out the unveiling of the greatest mystery of all, namely,

...what God determined as the way to bring out his best in us, long before we ever arrived on the scene. The experts of our day haven't a clue about what this eternal plan is. If they had, they wouldn't have killed the Lord of glory' – Jesus! There it is: God has always wanted to bring out his best in us. (1 Corinthians 2:7-8)

When world leaders do not recognise their profound ignorance about God's place and purpose for every person, impotence prevails. It is a helplessness of epidemic proportions. But just as he did in his Son, the man Jesus of Nazareth, God wants to 'bring out his best in us.' And when that revelation pervades us, we cannot miss out and neither can this present age. God has entrusted to us, his church in the world, something of his responsibility for the healing of his creation.

The church is a gathered group of people, whether small or great, through whom God wants to display his beauty and character. But he is adamant that church does not get lost in a self-serving mission.

John of Patmos laid a powerful challenge at the feet of a church in the first century, and circulated it for all the churches in the area to read and hear. It was a message for a vibrant church with a name and a reputation, bearing the marks of a place worth being involved with. However, what it looked like from the outside and what it was on the inside were two very different pictures.

These issues were apparently unnoticed by the leaders, nor discerned by the prophets or the intercessors. But the entire church was called to account before the one who sees everything.

I see what you've done, your hard, hard work, your refusal to

quit. I know you can't stomach evil, that you weed out apostolic pretenders. I know your persistence, your courage in my cause, that you never wear out. But you walked away from your first love— why? What's going on with you, anyway? Do you have any idea how far you've fallen? A Lucifer fall!

Turn back! Recover your dear early love. No time to waste, for I'm well on my way to removing your light from the golden circle. (Revelation 2:2-5)

Did you notice the unqualified indictment laid at the feet of this church about walking away from her first love?

No specifics are added about prophecy, preaching, biblical exposition, worship, praying, healing, evangelism, community work with the marginalised, or social justice. These would seem to be valid expressions of healthy church life. But the message was that even with such reputable statistics, something was missed entirely.

A church or Christian can look outstanding on the outside, winning the accolades and applause of many, and yet be found wanting because they have walked away from their first love. When our first love is Jesus, we are in a far better place to hear what God is saying about what he wants to do with us and his church. Any focus on our ministry, family or our business must not take precedent over Christ. Because there can only ever be one first love, and that is Jesus.

The question, 'O God, will I really make it?' must be examined in the light of this indictment. If the honest truth is that we have walked away from our first love, then we are choosing to say to God, 'I do not want you to be at home in me.' If we choose to remain unmoved by the Spirit's speech, regardless of how many good works we do, how skilful our musicianship is, how many diplomas in ministry we may acquire, or how big is the business we build to contribute to worldwide mission, they will be bereft of God's empowering presence.

When our first love is Jesus, all the things mentioned above can find their true place and priority. But if we are less than tenacious about cultivating this love, then all the things that we do for God will have a hollow ring. 'So no matter what I say, what I believe, and what I do, I'm bankrupt without love,' and especially love for Jesus.

Hear again the Spirit's speech to the church at Ephesus:

...But you walked away from your first love—why?

What's going on with you, anyway?

Do you have any idea how far you've fallen? A Lucifer fall!

Turn back! Recover your dear early love.

No time to waste, for I'm well on my way to removing your light from the golden circle.

It is when we get that sorted out, that we can live radically and daily, fully alive and alert to heaven's values transforming earth's reality. Our eyes need to be opened to see that all creation is waiting on tip-toe. Every living, breathing creature can be expectant and animated in worship of God. Then all else, even rainbows, will pale into insignificance.

Heaven must be grasped not merely as something far away, but as intrinsically within us, daring for expression in our flesh and blood existence, here and now. Indeed, this heaven-earth reality becomes powerfully actualised through us as vessels filled and overflowing with the life of the Holy Spirit. For it is his primary intention to keep us in love with Jesus and living a life without compromise which imitates him.

'This world is not my home; I am just passing through.' Intrinsic to believing this truth, is availing ourselves of the empowering presence of God. Then the world will see people gloriously and freely reflecting the image and character of the God who makes homeless humanity his home. Fatherless children find their perfect Father in Abba.

God is certainly big enough to handle everything. And from the very beginning when we entered into this profoundly personal relationship, God has shown himself as more than capable to make his home in us forever.

Home...

Over the years I have observed many people in international airports as they are getting ready to board a plane. They reflect a myriad of images and stories. However, the moment you enquire as to where they are headed, their faces change. The jaded frustration and imperfect scenarios from their travels now appear to fade. Particularly when they are returning home, there is a world of difference.

Be it homecoming reunions or, for that matter, reconciliations, just the thought of your own bed, that beautiful view or that special someone; that dearly loved pillow awaiting your return...even the gravity of anticipating the death of a loved one, but at least the privilege of being there at their side...there is something about home.

Of all the things that 'home' represents and reflects, it is about being and belonging. To be at home connotes belonging in the most sublime sense. We can make new homes away from where we were born, but conversations come to life when it comes to news about our primary origins. There are spirited conversations, comparing and contrasting foods and fads, cars and climate, politics and personal issues; home is connectedness. It is simply unavoidable.

Why do we both dread and crave a reunion?

Why do we love true stories of people finally connecting after many long years apart?

Why are we enamoured with letters written during the war years which are then recovered so that families can recall who so and so was in the picture that had pride of place on the mantelpiece?

Why do we unravel when we hear a loved one's voice through his handwritten correspondence?

Why do we love all that sort of stuff?

Because it is us deep down...

'O God, will I really make it?' takes on a whole new outlook when we see it in the context of the God who is beyond us and yet within us. He has come to inhabit our flesh-and-blood humanity. He wants to wear our skin so that he can continue to love this world into a place which will reflect his nature and his image. This is his longing.

Longing

The sense of longing transcends the physical and geographical; it reaches us in ways which defy mere logic. In old English, langian, the root of the verb 'to long' conveys the sense of 'to yearn for,' meaning 'to seem', or 'be', or 'grow long'. Strangely enough it is suggestive of the impersonal. It is not so much, 'I long for', but more literally, 'it longs me', whatever it might be. Therefore I would like to suggest that there is something about longing which differentiates it from wanting or desiring a thing.

Wanting is clear, urgent, driven by the will, with its goal clearly in view. By contrast, longing is something which does not originate between us and another thing. It is not directed by will, and its ultimate goal is not acquisition. Instead, it arouses in us a desire for union, or even re-union. It remains in the realm of the intuitive, and is often more spiritual in nature.

Like melancholy, spiritual longing has a drawn-out, reverberating quality. It is experienced as an elastic tension between the one who is longing and the object of that longing. The pull and tautness are like a bow string holding together the two ends of the bow that are never really separate.[2]

Think of Odysseus's longing – the original 'nostalgia' – nostos meaning 'the return home' and algos 'pain' for his native Ithaca. The thought of home apprehends Odysseus with every step he takes, in every dream, with every goblet of wine which fails to slake his thirst, with every ocean wave that brings him nearer to his heart's rest. His longing to ravish Penelope, the wife of his youth, to be intoxicated once again with their oneness, speaks of home. Longing is full of mixed emotions, painful and bittersweet.

This longing is articulated with furious passion by the Psalmist David. He employs the imagery of a deer searching for water in the arid inhospitable terrain of Palestine.

As the deer pants for streams of water,
so my soul longs after You, O God.
My soul thirsts for God, the living God.
When can I go and meet with God? (Psalm 42:1-2, NIV)
Or from The Message translation:
A white-tailed deer drinks from the creek;
I want to drink God, deep draughts of God.
I'm thirsty for God-alive.
I wonder, 'Will I ever make it— arrive and drink in God's presence?'
(Psalm 42:1-2)

Ostracised from public worship, David is soul-sick. His priority was not comfort or position; instead, he had a deep thirst for communion with God. It was an absolute necessity, like water to a parched traveler in the desert who alarmingly discovers the wells are dry; he must drink or die. Longing for David registers resolve; he must have his God or expire. His soul, his very self, his deepest life, was insatiable for a sense of the divine presence.

And much deeper than we can fathom, is God's deeper magic, which profoundly arrests and awakens us. The world which we inhabit is filled with uncertainties, risks and enigmas which defy human comprehension and there is so much which is outside our control. Eternity stalks us, confronting and confounding us, with glimpses of life beyond life and the things which really matter.

My dear friend David Shearman says that we were always meant to be 'presence carriers' as God's beautiful workmanship. This conveys to me the generous signal that God loves it when we find our rest in him, perhaps for the very first time. This homecoming to God answers our longings and immerses us in our true place of being and belonging. Fragmented people find their true healing and wholeness in the environs of him who is perfect love.

I am not speaking primarily and only about heaven in the next life. We live our lives with heaven as the final destination, but we also live now with God who is our ultimate home. It is not an either-or prospect, it is a both-and reality, celebrating heaven coming to earth. At the same time, we are on tip-toes, eager to be in the glorious new earth and the new heavens with God ultimately and forever.

Home is heart and head work

We cannot make God an object; God is not a thing to be named. We cannot turn God into an idea: God is not a concept to be discussed.

We cannot use God for making or doing: God is not a power to be harnessed.[3]

These words are disarming. God does not exist for me and my happiness. Without a shadow of doubt it takes a lifetime to learn how to truly forget about ourselves, daily letting go of everything that confines us to our personal universe. And even as we congratulate ourselves on being humble and honest, we find just how fleeting humility and honesty can be.

Being at home with God lands us squarely in the domain of relationship, where we can know and be known by another person. Within the Christian tradition we celebrate being known by God and knowing God, not as an object to be studied, nor as an idea to be analysed, nor as an entity house-trained to serve us.

God far exceeds these things. Home is where the one who is perfect love, perfects his work in our hearts as well as our heads.

Homes are of course buildings, but buildings do not become a home in isolation; homes are made. Some people are good at homemaking but the main work is not hanging curtains, painting and decorating, or choosing furniture. Homemaking is heart work. In a sense, to be, we need to be home, where our heart belongs. When a place to belong is assured, the adventure of growth can begin with great promise so that we do not lose our way.

I am at home when I allow God to perfect in me his character and empower me in the venture of becoming more and more truly human. This humanness transcends the unholy trinity of 'me, myself, and I.' I am a mere mortal, so plagued with corruption and selfish aspirations to be 'god,' yet I can be embraced, enveloped and immersed in God's presence.

His presence, living, laughing, loving in us was always what he had intended. We are not to be moulded by this world, but to live in it with our heavenly citizenship. God with us and God for us and God in us, living like Jesus. Where the robust presence of God is at work, there is no diminishment of the dignity of a human life. God's presence with us makes sense of what it means to be truly human.

Practically speaking, this translates into being fully present to one another, which can only happen when we first learn to be present to the Holy Other. Humanity can never transcend its present existence without the empowering presence of its true creator. It is his indwelling that illumines his image through me to a lost world filled with illusion. Rudolph Otto says that when someone has an authentic experience of the Holy, they find it at the same time 'a scary mystery and a very alluring mystery.'[4]

We both draw back from and are pulled forward into a kind of liminal space where we are not at home at all and yet totally at home, for perhaps the first time.

So where do we begin...?

If what I have been saying about God's intent to be at home with us has caught your attention, then the focus must remain with Jesus. Therefore we find ourselves back where it all started...

As he preached he said, 'The real action comes next. The star in this drama, to whom I'm a mere stagehand, will change your life. I'm baptizing you here in the river, turning your old life in for a kingdom life. His baptism – a holy baptism by the Holy Spirit – will change you from the inside out.' (Mark 1:7-8)

From my university days I was fascinated by the enigmatic figure of John the Baptizer. John appeared to be a man who was free from his own ego. He exemplified someone who was not trying to gather a following, but able to point beyond himself.

That day at the river Jordan, the crowds had gathered, but everything was going to change because of Jesus. Israel was standing at the brink of something very large indeed. John said, 'The real action comes next. The star in this drama, to whom I'm a mere stagehand, will change your life...'

John announced the climax of Israel's history, with the arrival of her Messiah. Jesus' arrival would mean an overturning of everything which had so defined Jewish identity and destiny. However, Jesus' vocation and mission would be expressed in ways that the nation of Israel could never have imagined. His life, work, death and resurrection would accomplish all of this in a radical way that would far transcend all the old categories.

When we first meet Jesus in the world of the gospels, it is Jesus as a Jew. And as a Jew, his life was influenced by not only the symbols of the Jewish world, but also by imperial Roman rule. Temple and Torah comprehensively governed Jewish life, identity and destiny, and yet all was under the overarching presence of Rome. And even for Jesus, politically speaking, Caesar was Lord.

Politics, religion, economics and social life were all enmeshed. For all Jews, maintaining their Jewishness was uppermost in their daily life. Underneath it all, they carried a heavy burden of unfulfilled promises from their own Hebrew Scriptures, while chafing under foreign overlords. Home's brightness was always eclipsed by the menacing shadow of Rome. To a degree, exile continued and Israel was not home.

The Jewish people knew that they must be fastidious in maintaining their loyalty to God. Crucial to their sense of identity and destiny was holiness, the distinctive which set them apart from every other people group on the earth. For both their present and future, holiness was the key to determining that they truly belonged to God.

Institutional holiness or interior holiness...

Prior to the coming of Jesus, there were a number of movements addressing the question of identity, 'Who are we? To whom do we belong?' Each group sought to give their own spin on what constituted a good Jew; understanding that theology affected everything that had to do with life. For a Jew the heart of their life was the Temple, out of which flowed their life source.

Long before any Christian holiness movements existed, in the first century world, two distinct holiness groups were prominent, each with their own specific proof texts to justify their existence and practices. Their fundamental, common denominator was that 'holiness' meant separation.

The first group were the Pharisees

The key verse of the Pharisaic movement was: *'I am holy, therefore you are to be holy, says the Lord God'* (Leviticus 19:1-2). What could be better than to have your movement aligned with the very character of God? Being a good Jew was inseparably related to becoming more like the God whom you served and worshiped.

The very name Pharisees or Hasidim conveyed the meaning of 'separated ones.'

Temple life was largely regulated by the Pharisees to maintain the holiness of life, in an institutional sense. Everything found its focus in the Temple: forgiveness of sins, ritual washings for uncleanness and purification. It represented the place of God's dwelling, where worshippers could encounter the presence of God, his Shekinah glory. The word 'Shekinah' symbolised 'the dwelling' or 'to inhabit,' and was actually used instead of the word 'God.' Because of the expectation that God was manifestly present in the Temple, holiness was a prerequisite for worshippers.

The second group were the Essenes

This monastic community of Essenes were devout Jews who were disenchanted with all that related to the Temple holiness movement. This is why Isaiah's words catapulted them into separating themselves from Jerusalem and the Temple, and saw them heading off to the wilderness at Qumran:

Thunder in the desert! 'Prepare for God's arrival! Make the road straight and smooth, a highway fit for our God...Then God's bright glory will shine and everyone will see it, Yes, just as God has said'. (Isaiah 40:3-5)

Above the Dead Sea, these fervent followers of Yahweh sculpted out a new community with very strict entrance requirements. Stern discipline regulated the spirit of the community: asceticism, rigorous study, and exacting precision in copying the Scriptures; rules about speaking, ritual purity; training in discernment and all manner of things pertaining to intense spirituality. The community of Essenes had withdrawn from the wicked world, espousing an interior holiness.

The Essenes' separation into the wilderness enabled them to play out the grand narrative of Isaiah's clarion call to exiled Israel.

Similar to the temple holiness movement of the Pharisees, their focus was initially good and nationalistic. However, it too became grossly myopic and prejudiced in its rigidity.

Appalled by the immorality and violence of Jerusalem, the corruption of the temple and its priesthood, and the compromise of religious leaders collaborating with the Romans, they simply packed their bags and withdrew to the wilderness to 'Prepare for God's arrival...make a highway fit for our God.' They called themselves the 'sons of light', but they failed to let their light shine, and their salt was as useless in their ghetto as the deposits on the shores of the nearby sea.

Counter punching

Each group sought avidly to preserve their God-given identity and destiny among the neighbouring nations. First-century Palestine was drenched with the mood of revolution. Subversives were watched as temple and wilderness movements propagated their particular brand of holiness. Nationalism and the intense maintenance of all things Jewish inflamed each group with 'holy' conviction in the recruitment of new members. However, Jesus' coming meant that nothing would ever be the same again in relation to holiness, identity, and destiny.

The Torah was in some groups elevated to such a place that the words of God were worshiped rather than God, but Jesus did not come to eliminate the Torah. Neither were the Essenes avowedly disloyal to the cause of all things Jewish. However, though both groups were fiercely loyal to Yahweh, their interpretation of the sacred texts suffered in motive and method. Jesus' arrival immediately caused a series of counterpunches which not only knocked down categories of thinking but especially, overturned how these groups saw 'kingdom come on earth as it is heaven.'

What each group held dangerously in common was the notion

of being 'right.' Personally, I have struggled with this issue for many long years. The one noticeable characteristic of the individual who believes that they are right is that their posture is predominantly defensive. Discussion is permitted but disagreement is frowned upon. Outwardly, words and concepts are exchanged, but more heat is generated rather than light.

However when disagreement can be tolerated by both sides, it creates a generous space for further on-going interaction. When both parties recognise being on a steep learning (and unlearning) curve, neither of them feel the need to prove or protect. On the keyboard of a piano, it is the space in between where the music is made. Maturing people are those who are able to celebrate the freedom of others to be themselves with their own vision.

I am not being entirely dismissive of truth which addresses harmful behaviour. Even cigarettes have a warning: Smoking is a health hazard. However, we may need to see that truth is also dangerous when used to exploit and distort the minds of others in the name of God.

Churches and church leaders too, must be careful that the outcome they are after is not merely number crunching and statistics. Or for that matter, that being a part of our group means that we are 'right' and have the 'right answers.' The domain of rightness and truth originates and flows from God. It is in relationship with him that we become humble recipients of whatever light he chooses to shed along the way.

The two holiness groups also believed that they had the monopoly on how God would bring about his kingdom rule over the foreign overlords. Their conviction was shaped by their critical interpretation of their much loved Scriptures. They staunchly believed that they would be involved and also fittingly blessed in restoring Israel to her place of prominence and entitlement.

A thirst for first things - Holy Spirit baptism

It all makes sense to me that if the Jews were so adamant in maintaining their identity as it related specifically to being 'holy' like God, then John's announcement: 'I'm baptizing you here in the river, turning your old life in for a kingdom life. His baptism – a holy baptism by the Holy Spirit – will change you from the inside out' – was not only strange, subversive speech, but also, compelling to say the least, especially with the emphasis on 'holy'! To speak of 'a holy baptism by the Holy Spirit' would surely command attention.

Baptism

The language of 'baptism' was clearly a first. In the Hebrew Scriptures we find the language of washings, purifications and ritual ablutions in the context of Temple and Levitical regulations, but not specifically, the word 'baptism.' In the context of the New Testament we need to grasp afresh that baptism symbolized death. Consider this conversation between Jesus and his disciples:

James and John, Zebedee's sons, came up to Jesus, 'Teacher, we have something we want you to do for us.' 'What is it? I'll see what I can do.' 'Arrange it,' they said, 'so that we will be awarded the highest places of honour in your glory—one of us at your right, the other at your left.' Jesus said, 'You have no idea what you're asking. Are you capable of drinking the cup I drink, of being baptized in the baptism I'm about to be plunged into?' 'Sure,' they said. 'Why not?' (Mark 10:35-40)

It was as if Jesus was saying, 'Are you boys certain about your readiness to die?'

This is not only about physical death, but something that will go on for the rest of your life, dying to everything which would keep you in the driver's seat and hogging centre stage! To submit to baptism means letting go of all that shapes your worldview about God and people and eternal matters. It is embracing death, to bring about a resurrection into the likeness of who God had always wanted you to be and what he wants to do with you.

The disciples' attempt to acquire positions of honour underscores the fact that they had no understanding of Jesus' words about 'the cup' and 'the baptism.'

Holy Spirit

Similarly, the words 'Spirit' or 'Spirit of God' are plentiful in the Hebrew Scriptures, and yet there are only three instances of the specific phrase, 'Holy Spirit' (Psalm 51:10; Isaiah 61:9,11). And none of these references is clearly identified with 'baptism.' Therefore its use invites us to see things differently about Jesus' coming and what it means to be the people of God. So what bearing does the Holy Spirit have on God being at home with us?

What counts is your life

John was adamant that Jesus and not he would be the one who baptises with the Holy Spirit. Jesus came to thoroughly overhaul all that had shaped them as Jewish worshippers. Yes, it started with John, but it finishes with Jesus. Every aspect of their lives would be impacted, especially that which related to the issue of holiness, and their identity and destiny as the people of God.

So what would Jesus initiate in terms of holiness and the Holy Spirit? And notice that none of the gospel accounts related to the baptizing activity of Jesus with the Spirit refers to the charismatic expression of glossolalia, prophecy, healings or any other gifts normally associated with the 'baptism of the Holy Spirit.'[5]

When a person has experienced the dynamic activity of the Holy Spirit, it is little wonder that there will be an overflow of speech or vision, or ecstatic, exuberant expressions of love. So by wrestling with the issues of holiness, identity and destiny as John and Jesus saw them, we might find another way of viewing Holy Spirit baptism in the overall purposes of God for Jews and Gentiles. And this will affect the response to our question, 'O God, will I really make it?'

Jesus, the 'true light that enlightens every person in the world,' was bringing an entirely new way of seeing, which would have profound implications for what it means to be at home with God. We need to critique our own perspective if we are to see the truth that illumines our understanding. Beginning a relationship with God sets us up for learning how to live.

Like Jesus, in true prophetic form, John pulled no punches. He certainly wasn't into winning popularity polls. The gospels present us with a clear picture as to the make-up of the crowds that gathered as we see them in both Matthew's and Luke's narratives.

When crowds of people came out for baptism because it was the popular thing to do, John exploded: 'Brood of snakes! What do you think you're doing, slithering down here to the river? Do you think a little water on your snakeskins is going to deflect God's judgment? It's your life that must change, not your skin. And don't think you can pull rank by claiming Abraham as 'father.' Being a child of Abraham is neither here nor there – children of Abraham are a dime a dozen. God can make children from stones if he wants. What counts is your life. Is it green and blossoming? Because if it's deadwood, it goes on the fire. (Luke 3:7-9)

The wet and the dry

For those who gathered, essentially there were two choices: hiding behind their place of entitlement – I am a Jew, I am of Abraham – or letting go and leaving behind what had defined their identity and destiny – now, I am a follower of Jesus.

This would be demanding in the extreme. Two groups would be readily identifiable: the wet and the dry. Both groups were making a statement. Those who had submitted to John's baptism, the wet heads, would be saying that they were ready for the change he spoke about:

The star in this drama, to whom I'm a mere stagehand, will change your life. I'm baptizing you here in the river, turning your old life in for a kingdom life. His baptism – a holy baptism by the Holy Spirit – will change you from the inside out. (Mark 1:7-8)

Of course, they like us really had no idea what they were getting themselves into with Jesus. No one has it all worked out, only God does. That is precisely why God remains God. This is neither negative nor inaccurate, it is simply keeping us on our toes when it comes to understanding who is really in charge.

The dry heads were unwilling to submit to John's baptism. They had settled into their entrenched position and tradition, as John had anticipated: 'We are of Abraham. There is no need for change.'

What God has been after all along is an inside job. If we are not changed from the inside out, we will never make it all the way. 'It's your life that must change, not your skin...God can make children from stones if he wants. What counts is your life.' Racial identity and kingdom destiny were redefined because of Jesus, as the apostle Paul proclaimed to his Jewish kinsmen and Gentile neighbours:

In Christ's family there can be no division into Jew and non-Jew, slave and free, male and female. Among us you are all equal. That is, we are all in a common relationship with Jesus Christ. Also, since you are Christ's family, then you are Abraham's famous 'descendant,' heirs according to the covenant promises. (Galatians 3:28-29)

This does not mean that those identity markers are eliminated, but it is putting everything in its proper place. What had once defined us before we met Jesus must now be subservient to him, who is Lord and Master of our lives. Everything is turned upside down, that is, the right side up.

From this vantage point, we now have the ability to begin seeing things entirely differently. Retaining the old identity markers as our primary reference points will suck the very life out of our faith venture with Jesus. He asks us constantly, 'Do you see what I see?'

Does our way of seeing inspire us to celebrate our new identity and new destiny in Jesus? Or are we still clinging to the old, only choosing some of the new things that Jesus holds out to us? Living in the Holy Spirit is entirely and thoroughly new. He is either Lord of all or not at all...

Jesus: we know who you are...

When Jesus came, his arrival and identity were veiled and puzzling to many, even his own disciples and his own people.

He was in the world, the world was there through him and yet, the world didn't even notice. He came to his own people but they didn't want him. (John 1:10)

Despite all the activity by the Jordan with the crowds, absolutely no one really grasped what John was saying about who Jesus is. Nonetheless, something quite shocking occurred, forcing Jesus to be exposed for who he was. Did it come about through the holiness campaigners – the Pharisees and the Essenes jointly exposing Jesus in order to expel him from their midst?

After all, these leaders who advocated temple (institutional) holiness and desert (interior) holiness had programs to protect, and members to maintain and recruit. And yet, strangely enough, neither brand of 'holiness' transformed the people of Jesus' day. What was offered by both groups was an onerous burden.

But there was one group who had actually grasped what the impact of Jesus' coming into the world of first-century Palestine would mean to them because they had experienced the power of holiness first hand. Mark tells us this story.

When the Sabbath arrived, Jesus lost no time in getting to the meeting place. He spent the day there teaching. They were surprised at his teaching – so forthright, so confident – not quibbling and quoting like the religion scholars. Suddenly, while still in the meeting place, he was interrupted by a man who was deeply disturbed and yelling out, 'What business do you have here with us, Jesus? Nazarene! I know what you're up to! You're the Holy One of God, and you've come to destroy us!' (Mark 1:21-24)

Loud and clear, not garbled and stammering, 'We know who you are – you're the Holy One of God...' Jesus in his human form is recognised by the powers of darkness as holiness personified, holiness embodied. Holiness finds its best and truest expression in Jesus. That description hurled at Jesus is remarkably similar to what was coined by Isaiah centuries before, about Yahweh, 'You are the Holy One.' Now this name is associated with Jesus, present on the human stage.

But according to Mark's narrative, 'You are the Holy One' is not uttered by the mouths of prophets nor from worshippers in praise, but from the hosts of darkness. It was the minions of evil forces. They knew only too well what the coming of Jesus would mean for the history of humanity, the entire world and the world to come.

The demonic outburst in the meeting place draws our attention, not only to the fact that this holiness would be something which the world had never seen before, but that it would also bring about the utter demise of the kingdom of darkness. When God is at home in us, darkness need no longer bind us up, so the answer to the question 'O God, will I really make it?' is a resounding yes. This is especially so, when Jesus is able to be fully alive in us, not for one day, three years or a generation, but for eternity!

Separation and differentness

If that were not enough, let's also capture the impact that Jesus' holiness had on the Pharisees and the Essenes. Both groups were deeply entrenched in the idea that holiness equalled separation. Jesus unquestionably overturns this definition. He places holiness squarely in the domain of differentness. And yet this differentness was about desirability, not detachment.

Jesus' holiness was not something austere and unattainable, but rather, it was about accessibility: accessibility both to God and for humanity. Holiness in humanity is about wholeness.

This beauty of wholeness has a powerful impact on both the darkness and the overtly religious. It means God – the Holy One – living in us, his holy temple. It is the beauty of God bringing out his best, clothed in human beings, which he chooses to wear before a watching world.

We are called to love God with our whole being as we enter into a relationship with him. It is distinctly a call toward wholeness, in stark contrast with the divided world we often inhabit and to the divided selves we often witness.

There is war, greed, enormous abundance for a few, and shortage and scarcity for many. And we are often at conflict with ourselves, with our world, our neighbour, and those who have made us enemies and those we make our foes. We say one thing but do another, or say something else that contradicts it. We deceive one another; we're not honest in our relationships with family, friends, or even with ourselves.

We are split in pieces when we are overwhelmed with tragedies, illness and death. We feel disjointed, out of place, not ourselves, disintegrated, and fragmented. Our friends and family might even tell us, 'You need to get it together,' when they see us falling apart. Wholeness is being at home in Jesus. And God by his Spirit is eager to continue this pattern in us, as he did in the life of his Son. For it is Jesus who stands first in the line of humanity he has restored (Romans 8:29-30).

Accessibility

What Jesus is saying to our divided selves and this divided world, is...'I am here for you. Allow me to wash your wounds; to heal your broken heart. As you touch my scars, allow me to touch your scars. Your scars, like mine, are permanent. You will see that I can be totally at home with you; welcome home to my heart.'

This wholeness could also be expressed as infectious holiness, which invades the disease, without being affected by it. Jesus' holiness overthrew the forces of darkness, to make them scream and go running:

'What business do you have here with us, Jesus? Nazarene? I know what you're up to! You're the Holy One of God and you've come to destroy us.' (Mark 1:23-24)

Picture this scene: an unnamed man who has tried to heed the Torah's instructions most of his life as he has attended the local synagogue. As Jesus walks in, this man encounters the Holy One. Light pierces the darkness and exposes the terrible torment within.

No other brand of holiness offered in the first-century Mediterranean world could deliver this man from his resident evil. Only Jesus would, could and can deliver anyone from their inherent lostness from God. Jesus enables people to return home to God.

Until the time when we were mature enough to respond freely in faith to the living God, we were carefully surrounded and protected by the Mosaic Law. The law was like those Greek tutors, with which you are familiar, who escort children to school and protect them from danger or distraction, making sure the children will really get to the place they set out for. (Galatians 3:23-24)

When we begin to see what it means to have the Holy Spirit living inside of us, we will also learn to celebrate the freeing truth that God has not stinted on anything. He has pulled out all stops to bring about holiness and character reformation from the inside out. The Holy Spirit wants to get us to the place where God can be totally at home with us. We are setting out for a lifelong journey of change to be like Jesus.

We must beware of distractions, especially if they draw us into anything that keeps Jesus from being our first and only true love. Here, Paul drives us and the recipients of his letter back to baptism, so that we face the answer to the question of our final chapter, 'O God, will I really make it?'

But now you have arrived at your destination: By faith in Christ you are in direct relationship with God. Your baptism in Christ was not just washing you up for a fresh start. It also involved dressing you in an adult faith wardrobe – Christ's life, the fulfilment of God's original promise. (Galatians 3:25-27)

We have arrived at our destination. This is the beginning of all our beginnings, namely, being at home with God. Our first signpost in navigating the way home began with 'Where do I begin?' We found ourselves at the river Jordan with John's strange speech about Jesus: 'His baptism – a holy baptism by the Holy Spirit – will change you from the inside out.' God's intention all along was to bring out his best in us as he makes his home in us.

It's truly an inside job

Changing us from the inside out, God's strategy has not changed. He wants to be alive in flesh and blood, wearing our skin, working out his will and purposes in human tissue. Yes, we are flawed and imperfect – yet God's life in us gives him the most pleasure as we allow ourselves to be at one with him. We are at work with him and he is at work in us. True humanness can only be rightly understood from the perspective of God being at home with us. Christianity is truly an inside job.

Jesus' living, dying and rising again has now made the gift of the Holy Spirit available and accessible. This means that every person in Christ can now appropriate the gift of holiness as the Holy Spirit lives inside us. Holiness cannot be achieved through external keeping of the law or the intensification of ritual and spiritual disciplines. God has not called us to make ourselves perfect. He knows that these efforts cause us simply to fall in love with ourselves and not him.

But by shifting our focus from what we do to what God does, don't we cancel out all our careful keeping of the rules and ways God commanded? Not at all. What happens, in fact, is that by putting that entire way of life in its proper place, we confirm it. (Romans 3:31)

The rules have their place, but essentially, they cannot bring change in the same way as the Holy Spirit can reproduce his nature inside us. A relationship of cooperation with the Holy Spirit is pivotal to the dynamic of change within a person's life. As we co-operate, he is able to operate inside of us, producing holiness as wholeness.

However, while we are still fixated on protecting and proving who we are, we are still trying to make ourselves more acceptable to God, others and especially ourselves. This is when we are bound to the distressing question, 'O God, will I really make it?' As we allow the Holy Spirit to make his home in us, then and only then will we be able to celebrate 'finally living for the first time'[6]

Living in the world for God

The gift of the Holy Spirit was never intended to enable us merely to escape from the world we live in. We are empowered to live in this world. For that matter, our best expressions of spirituality are not merely and only about getting a position on the platform of a church or before a congregation. Neither are we to retreat like self-conscious chameleons to a monochrome field. Rather, just as Jesus was given to this world, so are we.

We are given to the world, not to take on its colour but to disclose the new heaven and earth reality now at home within us, reflecting the colours of God. This is now the sphere of our true existence. The Spirit within us empowers us to demonstrate through our lips and life that Jesus is in the driver's seat. The gift of the Holy Spirit was always intended to liberate us into our true humanity, not about acquiring an intense brand of spirituality.

If it is only about our private walk with God, then we actually forfeit the revelation which has been granted to us, and our new life in Christ would have no bearing upon anyone else. Being at home with God places us on the steep learning curve of increasingly becoming whole and unreservedly loved.

Self-effacing is not loss of self

The gift of the Holy Spirit to us is primarily about bringing Jesus to the world through us. The Holy Spirit is utterly self-effacing, and like Jesus, he came not to draw attention to himself, but rather to point everyone to the Father. This is the opposite of our desire to be seen and heard, known and recognised.

Living in the fullness of God is being empowered to be utterly human, giving expression to the reality which is within, to the world without. Centuries ago, God said

I'll call nobodies and make them somebodies;
I'll call the unloved and make them beloved... (Romans 9:25)

These words can only ever make sense as we allow ourselves to be lost in the love of God our Father, in the freedom which Jesus brings and in the wholeness which the Holy Spirit wants to reproduce in us – from nobody to being a somebody – from unloved to being love.

The gravity of these words must invade the deepest spaces in our lives. I have been crucified in Christ, but I am not left for dead. The mystery has been revealed...

Indeed, I have been crucified with Christ. My ego is no longer central. It is no longer important that I appear righteous before you or have your good opinion, and I am no longer driven to impress God. Christ lives in me. The life you see me living is not 'mine,' but it is lived by faith in the Son of God, who loved me and gave himself for me. I am not going to go back on that. (Galatians 2:20)

Our resurrection life becomes realised through the wonderful empowering presence of the Holy Spirit. The Father and Son knew just how much we need to live life, so we were given the gift of the Holy Spirit. And because we are not dependent upon our own limited resources, we can avail ourselves of all that is true of God the Spirit who has come to make his home with us.

How can we lose with a God like that?

So we who once were nobodies, now are somebodies; we were unlovable but are now loved. But to get the benefit of these changes, take note of the final comments from Jesus' brother James. Our relationship with God is not a temporary thing, because he has entrusted us with responsibility for a world that needs to recover life and wholeness from the inside out.

Wholly holy

You're cheating on God. If all you want is your own way, flirting with the world every chance you get, you end up enemies of God and his way. And do you suppose God doesn't care? The proverb has it that 'He's a fiercely jealous lover.' And what he gives in love is far better than anything else you'll find. (James 4:4-5)

Cheating...flirting...enemies of God...a fiercely jealous lover...such words not only apply to the private world of my heart and head, but also to my relationships. There is rivalry, hostility, infidelity but also God's tenacious loyalty. Although I am led by the Holy Spirit, I try to get back in the driver's seat, doing what I want and being thoroughly flirtatious with the world, worshipping the idols of my own reflection. And no matter how much I deny this, deep down I know otherwise.

This intense loyalty from the Holy Spirit is likened by James to a 'fiercely jealous lover.' The word picture is intentionally provocative, meant to stir us out of our complacent, lukewarm positions of compromise. When we are only loosely loyal to God, we keep secrets to ourselves and even masquerade our past under the guise of well-rehearsed Christian jargon. Instead, we can choose the audacious lifestyle of staying in love with the lover who has come to make his home in us, who is love unfailing.

James' words catch us out; they are so sharp and hard hitting. God knows that we can spend the course of our day going through the motions and yet be entirely absent to him. God is present but we have absconded. What had apprehended us, turning us around so that we wanted change from the inside out, is only a memory and not a miracle of grace.

Habit may still keep us attending church, but our actual experience of God fades as we lose our way. It is not a total flight from God, but a subtle feeding of appetites that reinforce our love for the things of the world. And when the world offers attractive solutions, it becomes increasingly easy to accommodate ourselves to its ways in order to achieve our ends. The fight is a tempestuous one.

Either we will remain vigilant to allow God to do what he wants with us, or we will court friendship with the world. The truth can get so easily lost, namely that God intensely longs for each of us to allow him to be at home in us. But if we permit stuff which does not contribute to his home building design, the consequences are real and devastating.

Expulsion and expectation

On August 21st 2012, I awoke at two-thirty am with extreme stomach pain. Immediately, I found myself with my head in the toilet bowl, 'bowing to the porcelain god.' The pain was excruciating as my temperature fluctuated from boiling hot to extremely cold. Try as I might, nothing was forthcoming in the most literal sense, and all I could do was wait.

Helpless, I had to allow my body to dictate what it wanted to do.

It recognised the presence of a foreign body, something that clearly did not belong and was making its presence felt. That very morning I had an appointment with an old friend of mine who had travelled from overseas. Yet no matter how much I entertained the idea of being there at eleven-thirty, my body kept telling me, 'You are not going anywhere.' Reluctantly, I yielded.

While I was prostrate on the bathroom floor, I could not help think about this question, 'O God, will I really make it?' took on a far larger reality. It was much more than a mild stomach bug. Of course, my bout of sickness pales into insignificance compared to others' health crises. Nevertheless what was in me was not at home in my body.

Every part of me felt that something alien was making its presence known and I could not believe just how strenuously my body fought to get it out. My body was insistently shouting, 'This does not belong here.' If I denied the pain, it would be accommodating the very thing that my body was saying, 'Reject!'

Learning to listen to our bodies and spirits should translate into bold strokes of obedience and humility in every dimension of our humanity. I realised that as followers of Jesus we need to be so much more alert to the things which we habitually accommodate. Like my body trying to reject the alien thing, we need to quickly expel behaviours which run contrary to what Jesus loves.

The very fact that my body is sensitive enough to insist that, 'This does not belong; this is not meant to be here,' challenged me. How much do I accept stuff that is 'alien' to God in me? I realised that over the years, much of my own 'soul sickness' has been because I stubbornly resisted the Holy Spirit directing my attention to what needed expulsion.

He who knows us so thoroughly wants to educate us about what really matters about living life in love with him. Otherwise we may fall into the same category of a Christian community in the ancient world:

I know you inside and out, and find little to my liking. You're not cold; you're not hot – far better to be either cold or hot! You're stale. You're stagnant. You make me want to vomit... (Revelation 3:15-16)

As repugnant as these words are, if the body says we need to vomit something in order to recover full health, how much more imperative it is when God tells us how he sees our life. This does not mean the end; instead, it can actually mean the beginning of the long haul of renovation and reclamation.

Admittedly, it will be costlier than you had anticipated and require much more time than you had planned for. But over the long haul it is well worth it, especially, if it means growing up and maturing in the things which really matter in doing life with God and others.

Essentially, this has bearing on being at home with God whom James says is a 'fiercely jealous lover.' He does not want us to get lost along the way. He wants us to keep on keeping in step with his Spirit.

Undivided devotion

The idea of a jealous God has a dissonant ring to our ears. We imagine an over-possessive husband driven by an irrational, paranoid fear. In a way, jealousy is a kind of fear; it is the fear of losing someone. And yet it is also about the pain of being left out of one's life, the acute feeling of pain at losing touch with someone we love because he or she has been stolen away by someone else.

When it comes to understanding God as fiercely jealous, the Hebrew word provides some further insight. The Hebrew word associated with 'jealous' (qanah) *'for I, the Lord your God, am a jealous God'* (Exodus 20:5a) conveys both positive and negative connotations, ranging from a righteous zeal to blind fury.

H.G. Peels suggests that it is always with the 'notion of an intense, energetic state of mind, urging toward action.'[7] Both in the context of Exodus and in James' letter, God's passionate zeal insists on possessing what rightfully belongs to him, namely humanity made in his image; humanity being at home with him.

This passionate concern arises out of God's holiness, as he longs for us to be saturated with his wholeness. Through the indwelling activity of the Holy Spirit we are now empowered with zeal, no longer for what we want but for what God wants. This is precisely why James objects to his audience and says:

And do you suppose God doesn't care? The proverb has it that 'he's a fiercely jealous lover.' And what he gives in love is far better than anything else you'll find.

God's holiness and jealousy all point to his fiery zeal to keep us from all that could destroy us and those around us, including our abortive attempts to ignore God's Spirit and throw our faith overboard.

Therefore we need not be anxious or alarmed by God's holiness. It should give us great comfort and reassurance that he will leave heaven and turn hell upside down to keep us from destroying ourselves. He does so in a way that does not violate our humanity or what is consistent with his character. He wants us to know that 'O God, will I really make it?' has already been answered.

Non dualism – both and

Our day and age affords us with a vast array of Bible translations. This essentially means that scriptures are made much more accessible to us so that we can pick up on the finer nuances of the original languages. The text I have in mind offers an array of meanings, but all focus clearly on understanding the role of God's Spirit in the life of a Christian. Let's look at some of the variations on James 4:5 about God's claim on us:

Or do you think the scripture means nothing when it says, 'The spirit that God caused to live within us has an envious yearning'?

179

(New English Translation)

Or do you suppose it is to no purpose that the Scripture says, 'He yearns jealously over the spirit that he has made to dwell in us'? (English Standard Version)

Or do you think Scripture says without reason that the spirit he caused to live in us envies intensely? (New International Version)

Do ye think that the scripture saith in vain, 'The spirit that dwelleth in us lusteth to envy'? (King James Version)

The Spirit which he has caused to dwell in us yearns jealously over us. (Weymouth New Testament)

And do you suppose God doesn't care? The proverb has it that 'he's a fiercely jealous lover.' And what he gives in love is far better than anything else you'll find. (James 4:5, The Message).

Just from this sampling of the texts, we can see why scholars over the years have had such difficulty in translating, interpreting and expounding James 4:5. And because 'spirit' in the Greek language is not in capitals, it is unclear whether James is alluding to the human spirit or the Holy Spirit. However, there is unity to be discovered even in this diversity as it relates to God's Spirit at home with us. Therefore in the final chapter I want to offer the following application.[8]

On the one hand, James may well be continuing to focus on the human spirit in relation to its capacity for destructive attitudes and behaviour. We can observe this in the verses which precede our text under investigation:

Where do you think all these appalling wars and quarrels come from? Do you think they just happen? Think again. They come about because you want your own way, and fight for it deep inside yourselves. You lust for what you don't have and are willing to kill to get it. You want what isn't yours and will risk violence to get your hands on it. You wouldn't think of just asking God for it, would you? And why not? Because you know you'd be asking for what you have no right to. You're spoiled children, each wanting your own way. You're cheating on God. If all you want is your own way, flirting with the world every chance you get, you end up enemies of God and his way. (James 4:1-4)

The human spirit certainly is exposed for its innate antagonism against God's love and light. However, if this was all that James was showing the believers, it would be quite a limited picture. Rather, if we see the dynamic presence of the Spirit of God dwelling in us, also jealously longing for our spirits to be at home with God, then we can see that James is offering an antidote, a remedy for our rebellion. In effect, it is not one or the other, it is both-and.

Home and heaven

Richard Weymouth's (1903) rendering, 'The Spirit which he has caused to dwell in us yearns jealously over us,' emphatically explains why God has always wanted to be at home in us. Eugene Peterson reminds us further that God is '"a fiercely jealous lover." And what he gives in love is far better than anything else you'll find.'

If God does not build the home, then without him involved in our lives, we are merely building a shack. His yearning is inflamed with fiery love to yield up from our lives a beautiful house for him and us to live in together.

What God gives will always far surpass anything that anyone could offer us. Change is inevitable, for that is the nature of repentance. For this is precisely where we first began in this venture with God and it will continue to the end. However, the moment we are through with changing, quite literally, we're through. C. S. Lewis captured this in his analogy of God the great renovator:

'Imagine yourself as a living house. God comes in to rebuild that house. At first, perhaps, you can understand what he is doing. He is getting the drains right and stopping the leaks in the roof and so on: you knew those jobs needed doing and so you are not surprised.

But presently he starts knocking the house about in a way that hurts abominably and does not seem to make sense. What on earth is he up to? The explanation is that he is building quite a different house from the one you thought of – throwing out a new wing here, putting on an extra floor there, running up towers, making courtyards. You thought you were going to be made into a decent little cottage: but he is building a palace.'[9]

His desire is never to tolerate anything which could destroy our relationship with him.

He is building a palace which will far exceed the Taj Mahal.

He is building a home out of living stones.

He is committed to giving us an absolutely amazing new beginning.

He is committed to working with us and in us all the way to the very end.

His love throughout our faith journey will far exceed anything that we had ever imagined.

So in the interim, this work is a co-operative effort with our part and his. And we must daily learn to welcome the truth of not only what we are, but whose we are and what we are living for. Ultimately all things will be brand new, ushering hope, energising faith, and informing our desire to make his work our priority. 'O God will I really make it?' is par for the course, as distractions will always be in our journey of faith.

But let me tell you something wonderful, a mystery I'll probably never fully understand. We're not all going to die – but we are all going to be changed. You hear a blast to end all blasts from a trumpet, and in the time that you look up and blink your eyes – it's over. On signal from that trumpet from heaven, the dead will be up and out of their graves, beyond the reach of death, never to die again. At the same moment and in the same way, we'll all be changed. In the resurrection scheme of things, this has to happen:

everything perishable taken off the shelves and replaced by the imperishable, this mortal replaced by the immortal. Then the saying will come true:

Death swallowed by triumphant Life!

Who got the last word, oh, Death?

Oh, Death, who's afraid of you now?

It was sin that made death so frightening and law-code guilt that gave sin its leverage, its destructive power. But now in a single victorious stroke of Life, all three – sin, guilt, death – are gone, the gift of our Master, Jesus Christ. Thank God! (1 Corinthians 15:51-57)

These claims are accurate and trustworthy. They explain truth that helps us live out our lives now as followers of Jesus. Just, as the Spirit of God was 'making himself at home with Jesus,' so he wants to make himself at home with us. Jealously, fiercely loving us all the way to when the new heavens and the new earth finally become ours as Father, Son and Holy Spirit had always intended!

It is inconceivable that we could bear the likeness of God or reflect his nature unless we had the empowering presence of the Spirit of God at home in us. If we can grasp the breath-taking thought that God had planned all along that we should be his dwelling place, then our hearts will be enlarged beyond our wildest notions to allow God to be in us, with us, for us and through us – at 'home' in us.

Anyone who claims to be intimate with God ought to live the same kind of life Jesus lived.

It's a mistake to fear that God will leave us when we mess up or fail him. God has come to be at home with us. He first met us at the cross, knowing the worst about us, and yet, he chose to reveal to us a love that is breathtakingly freeing.

We need to be fully alive and alert to ever-increasing wholeness becoming a reality, as we keep in step with the Spirit. This inside job plunges us into the fullness of God's purposes. Without embarrassment, we learn to live in love without measure.

Heaven is not lost in this equation; if anything it is even more realised. Being at home with God enables us to taste of the combined heaven-and-earth reality now. As we learn to be invaded by the living Spirit, God teaches us to trust him for all that is to come, when finally everything will make absolute sense:

I heard a voice thunder from the Throne: 'Look! Look! God has moved into the neighbourhood, making his home with men and women! They're his people, he's their God. He'll wipe every tear from their eyes. Death is gone for good – tears gone, crying gone, pain gone – all the first order of things gone.' The Enthroned continued, 'Look! I'm making everything new. Write it all down – each word dependable and accurate.' (Revelation 21:3-5)

In no uncertain terms, this imagery expresses not just a respite from all that has caused pain now, but it is clearly the end: 'Death is gone for good – tears gone, crying gone, pain gone – all the first order of things gone.'

Ultimately, home for every living creature is a place of permanence with God. There nothing will deny us the life God fully intended.

Look! Look! God has moved into the neighbourhood, making his home with men and women!

In our eternal home we will be derailed no more by our own self-conscious inclinations of heart and mind. 'O God, will I really make it?' has been wonderfully answered. We shall be all the more at home now, as we allow God to be God in us in his unending story.

Conclusion

Home is a celebration of oneness and dignity. Home is where the pain of the past is wiped away by the scarred hands of the wounded healer. Where past, present and future will be no more, eternity beckons us to drink deeply from him who is love immeasurable.

Home is where our faces are held high to see him who has known us and has made us to be with him forever. Then we can shout, 'We have finally arrived, we are there!'

Therefore in The Art of Not Getting Lost on the Way Home we must embrace the final truth that when God comes to us, it is to be at home now with us, and ultimately forever.

What we're trying to persuade people about is that the God we believe in is a God who never lets go of those he has made.

The God to whom all are alive because he has breathed life into them, and once he has laid his hands on their lives and left his imprint and breathed his breath – that relationship will never disappear.[10]

I am convinced that yes, we will ultimately make it. Because there is so much more to come from the One who above all else, wants me to know that he is completely at home in me as I learn to live in his unending love.

Endnotes

1. Please note: Mark 16:9-20 is contained only in later manuscripts.
2. See also, I. McGilchrist, *The Master and his Emissary: The Divided Brain and the Making of the Western World* (London: Yale University Press, 2010) 390-391.
3. Eugene Peterson, *The Pastor: A Memoir*, (New York: HarperCollins, 2011), 186.
4. Rudolf Otto, *The Idea of the Holy* (London: Oxford University Press, 1977), 39
5. When we think of the expression 'Baptism of the Spirit' what it meant in John's day and what it has come to mean now, are worlds apart. Moreover, the term is never a noun; it is always a verb 'baptised' rather than 'baptism'. Furthermore it only occurs 7 times in the entire New Testament. 6 of these are a repetition of John the Baptizer's utterance (Gospels and Acts) and, the final one is from Paul in 1 Corinthians 12:13
6. Matt Stinton and Jeremy Riddle, "This is what you do, you make me come alive", Loft Sessions, Bethel Music, 2012.
7. H. G. L. Peels, "qanah," Willem A. Van Gemeren, gen. ed., NIDOTTE (Grand Rapids: Zondervan, 1996), 3:938.
8. Please keep in mind there are numerous commentaries available and research papers accessible on this specific text.

9. C. S. Lewis, *Mere Christianity*, (New York: MacMillan Co., 1960), 160.
10. Sermon delivered by the Archbishop at Lichfield Cathedral during a visit to the diocese of Lichfield (7/11/10).

Conclusion

Fearing that we can be forgotten by God; struggling with how we get to know God intimately and personally without becoming know-it-alls; stumbling to work out what God is trying to tell us; even challenging, 'O God, is that really you?' and floundering over 'O God, will I really make it?' all bring formation as well as frustration in our relationship with God.

However, these questions direct us to remain engaged with God about everything, so that we do not get lost along the way. Whether or not we get answers, they help us stay the distance with Jesus who embodies truth in the most freeing sense of that word. In Jesus, we see that God is sticking with us from the beginning to the very end. Even death and hell cannot escape his attention when it comes to any person being alienated and lost from his love.

God knows that we do lose our way at times; it is par for the course. Our faith journey with Jesus brings us into the larger reality of what God has brought us into, a life which is utterly world changing. This is why staying the entire course in our human journey with God – just like Jesus – to the very end is primarily about learning to allow the Holy Spirit to make his home in us. It is not a short contract; it is a forever journey.

Anyone who loves me will obey my teaching. My Father will love them, and we will come to them and make our home with them. Anyone who does not love me will not obey my teaching. These words you hear are not my own; they belong to the Father who sent me. (John 14:23-24)

Jesus is concerned that we fully cooperate with the gift of the Holy Spirit. By doing this, we are giving permission for him to operate in us so that God can be at home in us. Living in the Spirit means bringing out God's best in us for a world that has yet to see the authentic beauty of wholeness.

It is a wholeness that is produced by God being at home in us.

It is a wholeness that finds its true expression in staying in love with Jesus.

It is a wholeness which increasingly becomes ours as we allow ourselves to be loved by the God who keeps telling us, 'You are chosen, marked by my love and pride of my life.'

Therefore in order to become skilled in the art of not getting lost on the way home, it is essential to allow love not only to overthrow all our fears, but also empower us with humility to keep on asking the questions which God is ready to hear. God is always there for us, so that love becomes at home and matures in us.

Do you remember where we first began with that old song?

But if heaven never were promised to me
Neither a land where I would live eternally
It's been worth just having the Lord in my life...

God is my home and being at home in him right now makes all the difference to this world and the next. Being at home with God transcends even the highest notion of what heaven may represent.

That is why our fears that we won't make it reveal how little we understand of God's long-range plans for us, for humanity, and for this world and the next.

Being at home with God right now, even in our imperfect lives, is finally living for the first time. That is why we don't have to get lost. Our present age needs to encounter people living out the twin reality of heaven and earth, right now, who are alive to God and all that God wants to make alive through us for others.

We have been brought to the one place where we will never be abandoned, rejected, or used. We have been captured by God and delivered to that space called home, where being and belonging eclipse any other notion of what it means to be truly human.

Our true beginning, our ending and everything in between all find their focus in Jesus. There is so much that the Father, Son and Holy Spirit want to show us about making an eternal home in us. It is as we remain in God's unending love that we realize it is the only environment conducive for us.

God wants to take us further into his love so that we may take others to their true home in him. Lostness is overtaken by being found, known and never ever having to entertain the thought of God saying goodbye to us.

'Meanwhile the joyful anticipation deepens' in this life and for the next as we venture forward. The art of not getting lost on the way is simply learning to be at home with God now and forever. After all, it was his idea in the first place and what he starts, he will always finish with the most consummate skill. Only God knows how to put his finishing touches to his masterpiece – humanity at home in him!

About the Author

Vangjel Shore was the head of New Testament Studies in the Garden City College, Brisbane, Australia from 2003-2009. He has a Masters in Theology from the University of Queensland where he also completed a PhD, "Ears to Hear in the Book of Revelation" in 2003. He has recently completed an extensive teaching ministry on the Gospels in the United Kingdom, Atlanta and Brasil in 2007.

Subsequently, in 2010, he has recently returned from a teaching and preaching ministry in the United Kingdom. He has also written a chapter entitled "The Titles of Jesus" under the supervision of Dr Mark Harding and Professor Alana Nobbs for the publication The Content and Setting of the Gospel Tradition by Eerdmans.

From 2009 he was appointed to the staff of Hillsong Brisbane Campus as Pastor of Spiritual Formation and in 2010 was involved in the Evening College Course as Co-Ordinator and Lecturer.

Currently Vangjel is Campus Director and Senior Lecturer in New Testament Greek and Spiritual Formation at the Australian Christian Churches AlphaCrucis College in Brisbane.

Find out more about Van's writing at:

http://www.conversationwithvan.jimdo.com